A Spiritual Pilgrimage to France

by Anne Richards Tschanz

Witness Ministries
825 S. Waukegan Road, PMB-200
Lake Forest, IL 60045

Nihil Obstat
Reverend Robert L. Tuzik, Ph.D.
Censor Deputatus
September 24, 2002

Imprimatur
Most Reverend Raymond E. Goedert, M.A., S.T.L., J.C.L.
Vicar General
Archdiocese of Chicago
October 7, 2002

The Nihil Obstat and Imprimatur are official declarations that a book is free of doctrinal and moral error. No implication is contained therein that those who have granted the Nihil Obstat and Imprimatur agree with the content, opinions, or statements expressed. Nor do they assume any legal responsibility associated with publication.

Publisher:
Witness Ministries
825 S. Waukegan Road, PMB-200
Lake Forest, IL 60045

Phone: (847)735-0556 * (866)WIT-NESS
FAX: (847)735-0911
Email: WitnessM@aol.com
www.witnessministries.org

ISBN: 1-892835-05-3

Cover: *St. Geneviève Watches Over the Sleeping City of Paris*, 1898 (oil on canvas) by Pierre Puvis de Chavannes (1824-98). Pantheon, Paris, France/Giraudon-Bridgeman Art Library.

Table of Contents

A Spiritual Pilgrimage to France

Preface

This book about French saints and holy places combines three things that I dearly love: the Catholic Church, history and travel. It was originally written as a booklet to accompany a Witness Ministries pilgrimage group to France, but I have since expanded it to include many more holy people and places.

I did not have any preconceived notions about how this book should be organized. When I learned that France is known as the "Eldest Daughter of the Church" because she was the first nation to embrace Christianity after the fall of the Roman Empire, it became apparent to me that I should begin with the people and places most closely associated with the introduction of Christianity to France. It also seemed fitting to end the book with the building of the Basilica of Sacré-Coeur because it symbolized to me the faith of the French people yesterday, today and into the future; a faith kept alive despite persecution, revolution and, in the modern age, secularism.

Throughout the course of centuries, France offered a special contribution to the Catholic Church, through the enlightened and heroic witness of her saints, the vigorous doctrine of her teachers and the apostolic courage of her missionaries.
—Pope John Paul II
France: Message of Peace, Trust, Love and Faith

Looking back over my life, I had more ties to France than I had at first realized. I attended St. Mary's College in Indiana, founded by the Sisters of the Holy Cross who came from Le Mans, France, in 1843, and I often prayed at the Lourdes Grotto at the University of Notre Dame. When I drifted away from the Church, it was Our Lady who guided me back and it was a priest from the La Salette Missionaries who heard my first confession in over ten years. After all of this, I became a confirmed pilgrim, traveling to La Salette, Lourdes, Chartres and every other French shrine I could find.

Tomb of Fr. Alphonse
Ratisbonne

In 1995, I took a sabbatical from my job at IBM to become a volunteer at Ecce Homo convent and pilgrim hospice in Jerusalem. The founder of Ecce Homo was Alphonse Ratisbonne, a Jewish Frenchman by birth who became a Roman Catholic priest in 1842 after he wore a Miraculous Medal and had a vision of Our Lady. I was surprised to find Alphonse's lonely grave in a Sisters of Sion cemetery outside of Jerusalem. In some mysterious way, I felt that my purpose in coming to Jerusalem was fulfilled in that moment. I came away with a determination to write about Alphonse and the many other French people who have contributed to the spreading of the Gospel. The seed that was planted then has borne fruit in *A Spiritual Pilgrimage to France.*

I thank Joan and Tom McHugh for giving me the opportunity to publish this book and I thank my dear husband Tom who has supported me faithfully throughout (and allowed many books to infiltrate our house). I have grown to love the people on these pages as if they were friends of mine. I hope they become part of your life as well.

May all the saints of France bless you.

Anne Richards Tschanz

Acknowledgements

I would like to thank: Peter Ptak, for helping a novice author through, not only the creative design of the cover and text, but also through the laborious process of correcting and amending the copy. His patience and diligence were beyond measure; Dan Gallio, for his multiple reviews of the text and for providing invaluable suggestions and comments that greatly added to readability and clarity; Joan and Tom McHugh, for trusting that a book such as this would be of value and interest to people and for encouraging me throughout the whole process; and to all those who gave nothing but unconditional support, especially my husband Tom and my family.

⚜ The Fleur-de-Lys ⚜

The fleur-de-lys, the symbols seen at the beginning of every chapter, was the ancient symbol adopted by the kings of France. There are many legends associated with the fleur-de-lys. One states that when Clovis, the King of the Franks, was trying to elude the Goths, he noticed some irises growing in the Rhine River indicating shallow water and a safe place to cross. He successfully escaped and the iris, adapted as the fleur-de-lys, became his emblem. Clovis' wife, St. Clotilda, prayed for his baptism to the Faith but her pleas were ignored. One day Clovis believed that his gods had abandoned him and he asked the Lord for help. He said, "Jesus Christ, you are proclaimed by Clotilda Son of the living God. You are said to give aid to those in distress and grant victory to those who hope in You. I entreat from a devout heart the glory of your help. If you grant victory over these enemies . . . then I will also believe in You and be baptized in Your name."[1] He was victorious and was baptized by St. Remi on Christmas Day in 496 AD. St. Remi told him, "Meekly bow thy proud head; adore that which thou hast burned, burn that which thou hast adored."[2]

The iris became intimately associated with the Christian kings of France and was used by King Louis VII in the twelfth century on his standard during a crusade, hence the name, fleur de Louis. Charles V portrayed the fleur-de-lys in groups of three to symbolize the Trinity.

✤ One ✤

Mary Magdalene

It may seem strange to talk about France and St. Mary Magdalene, but according to Provence tradition, her final resting place is in the Basilica in St-Maximin-la-Ste-Baume in southern France. Her bones, apparently hidden away in 716 to protect them from the Saracen invaders, were rediscovered in 1279 by Charles of Anjou, a brother of King St. Louis IX. The basilica and the cave where she spent the last years of her life became popular pilgrimage destinations in competition with Vézelay, which also claimed to have some of her relics.

The majority of the people who sought out the Savior did so to be cured of bodily diseases, not of spiritual maladies. Only the Magdalen, the great saint, came to Him that He might treat her heart and cure her spiritual infirmities.
—St. Francis de Sales
The Sermons of St. Francis de Sales for Lent

Mary Magdalene was the woman out of whom Jesus had driven seven demons (Mk 16:9, Lk 8:2). She is often called the "Apostle to the Apostles"

St. Mary Magdalene

because Jesus first appeared to her after the resurrection. While Mary wept outside the empty tomb, the Lord said to her, "Woman, why are you weeping? Whom are you looking for?" At first, Mary did not recognize Him. Then Jesus said to her, "Mary!" and she said to him in Hebrew, "Rabbouni." St. Louis de Montfort said that Jesus "spoke only one word—'Mary'—to the grief stricken Mary Magdalene and she was overwhelmed with joy and happiness."[1]

Blessed Elizabeth of the Trinity, a French Carmelite, longed to stay near Jesus in silent adoration as Mary Magdalene did. Elizabeth wrote, "Do you not have the same passionate longing to listen to him? At times, one feels so strongly the need of silence that one would wish to do nothing but remain like Mary at the Master's feet, eager to hear all, to penetrate ever more deeply into that mystery of charity which he came to reveal to us. Yet do you not find that in action, when we are apparently doing Martha's work, the soul can remain buried in its contemplation like Mary, staying near to him? . . . It seems to me that we must draw very close to the Master, commune with his soul, become identified with its every movement, and then go forth as he did to do the will of his Father."[2]

—Blessed Elizabeth of the Trinity

In western Provence is the city of Avignon where the papacy remained in exile for sixty-eight years from 1309-1377 during the so-called Babylonian Captivity. During the Great Schism which followed the return of the papacy to Rome, the magnificent Palace of the Popes, which appears to be more of a fortress than a palace, was the home of two antipopes.

Avignon is also the site of a Eucharistic miracle that occurred in 1433 at the Chapel of the Holy Cross. Two hundred years earlier, King Louis VIII came to the city to make public reparation for the sacrileges committed by the Albigensians, who denied the Real Presence. The Blessed Sacrament was carried through the city and, because of the enthusiastic reception of the crowds, the Bishop decided that the Eucharist should be perpetually exposed. In 1433, flood waters threatened the adoration chapel but, when members of a confraternity known as the Grey Penitents reached the chapel by boat, they found that the altar and all of the books, cloths and reliquaries were totally dry even though the waters inside reached to the height of four feet. The event was commemorated each year on November 30 until the French Revolution of 1789 when the chapel was destroyed. It was rebuilt in the 1800s as a chapel of perpetual adoration.

Mary Magdalene is sometimes said to be the sister of Martha and Lazarus as well as the penitent woman who washed Jesus' feet with her tears. Today, many Scripture scholars believe that these are separate women. Provence tradition states, however, that a boat carrying Mary Magdalene, Martha, Lazarus, St. Maximin and a slave, Sarah, among others, arrived at Les Stes-Maries-de-la-Mer near Marseilles following a persecution of the Christians. An oratory was built there and Sarah's relics, greatly revered by the gypsies, are said to be in the crypt of the church today. Martha went on to Tarascon where the Church of St. Martha lays claim to her relics. Lazarus' remains are thought to be in Autun in the church bearing his name.

Pope John Paul II recognized the antiquity of Christianity in France when he said, "Here, in France, the mission given by Christ to the Apostles after the Resurrection was very soon started, if not with certainty in the apostolic era, at least from the second century, with Irenaeus, the great martyr and apostolic father, who was Bishop of Lyons."[3]

Another unexpected saint whose remains are reputed to be in Provence is St. Anne, the mother of the Blessed Virgin Mary. According to tradition, Anne died in Jerusalem but her relics were carried to Provence and interred in Apt in the cathedral of Sainte-Anne. Charlemagne, the King of the Franks from 768-814, was a visitor to Apt in the eighth century and viewed the relics of St. Anne.

In Brittany, Sainte-Anne d'Auray is the site of pilgrimages in honor of St. Anne. In 1623, St. Anne appeared to Yves Nicolazic and asked that a chapel be built to replace a fifth century chapel. During the French Revolution, the shrine was ransacked but, in 1877, a new basilica was consecrated. According to the *Protoevangelium of St. James* (c. second century), Anne and her husband Joachim grieved over their lack of children. While Joachim prayed in the desert for forty days, an angel appeared to Anne and said, "The Lord has heard your prayer, and you shall conceive and bring forth, and your seed shall be spoken of in all the world."[4] Anne presented her child, Mary, as a gift to God. Anne is the patron saint of childless women and the principal saint of Brittany. Pope John Paul II visited the shrine in 1996.

According to tradition, Mary Magdalene evangelized Marseilles and Aix-en-Provence, spending the last years of her life in prayer in a cave at Sainte-Baume. Shortly before her death, Mary left the cave to receive a final Holy Communion from St. Maximin. To-

Reliquary of St. Mary Magdalene

day, her relics reside in a sarcophagus in the crypt of the Basilica of St. Maximin. Up in the mountains, her cave has been a pilgrimage site since at least the fifth century. St. Vincent de Paul, St. Francis de Sales, Ven. Charles de Foucauld and St. Louis were visitors to the site. King Louis XIII came to pray for an heir. His son, Louis XIV, came with his mother in thanksgiving.

Martha and Mary! The eternal conflict of material life and external existence with the imperishable needs of the soul; the call from without, pressing us to uncover the hidden forces of our soul, to abandon inner recollectedness for the activity that is more pure, more fruitful or so it seems. . . . (But) Mary triumphs; and if our bodies must often be given to the humble tasks of Martha, it is only on the condition that our soul, like Mary, devotes itself to the contemplation and adoration of Him who speaks the divine word, and that we know how to listen in silence to that word in the depths of ourselves. The worth of activity lies only in the meditation that has prepared it and in the offering of it to God.[5]
—Elisabeth Leseur

The cave at Sainte Baume was destroyed during the French Revolution but the sanctuary was rebuilt. Visitors are welcome to stay in a pilgrim house managed by the Dominicans. The most popular dates of pilgrimage are the feast day of Mary Magdalene on July 22 and Christmas Midnight Mass. It is impossible to know if these traditions are true, but it really doesn't matter. The faith brought by pilgrims over the centuries to these sacred sites has made them holy.

O St. Mary Magdalene,
you remained with the Lord during his death on Calvary
and were privileged to be a witness to the Resurrection.
May we too remain faithful to Jesus,
even when our spiritual trials are greatest,
knowing with certainty that the Lord is our Savior.
May you and the holy Apostles pray for us. Amen.

Prayer of Elisabeth Leseur[6]

(Elisabeth [d. 1914] has been called a "married St. Thérèse of Lisieux")

O my God,
through the precious Blood of Jesus and his five wounds,
grant me today five graces:
the conversion of a sinner;
the conversion of an unbeliever;
the salvation of someone dying in peril of everlasting death;
a vocation to the priesthood or to religious life;
and, for some new soul,
the grace of entering into and savoring
the mystery of the Eucharist. Amen.

✤ *Two* ✤

Notre-Dame de Fourvière

In the city of Lyons, high on a hill, is the famous shrine of Notre-Dame de Fourvière. The hill of Fourvière is sometimes called "the hill that prays" because of the churches, convents and monasteries that once occupied the site and the "hill of blood" for the Christian martyrs who died for the Faith in the Roman forum that was located in the area of the present basilica. But mostly, Lyons is known as the "City of Mary" for she has shown time and time again that she is protecting the city. Every December 8, the people of Lyons illuminate the city to honor their protectress.

Lyons was founded in 43 BC by the Romans who made it the capital of Gaul. Lyons was Christianized in the second century, evangelized by St. Pothinus and the slave St. Blandina, who were martyred there in 177 AD. Their remains are said to have been in the crypt of the Basilica of St. Martin-d'Ainay in Lyons. St. Irenaeus, a disciple of St. Polycarp who was, in turn, a disciple of St. John the Evangelist, followed Pothinus as bishop. Strangely enough, Herod Antipas and his wife, Herodias, who requested John the Baptist's head, died here in exile.

Notre Dame de
Fourvière

I have always had a special devotion to St. Blandina who was martyred at Lyons and whose life was written by Eusebius. Amidst all the excruciating torments of her martyrdom, she kept repeating gently, 'I am a Christian,' making use of this word as a sacred balm to heal all of her wounds.

—St. Francis de Sales
*The Sermons of St. Francis de Sales
for Advent and Christmas*

St. Pothinus erected the first shrine to Our Lady in Lyons, traditionally on the site now occupied by the church of St. Nizier. In the ninth century, a chapel was built over the ruins on the hill of Fourvière. When the chapel was enlarged in 1168, St. Thomas à Becket asked to whom it would be dedicated. The answer was, "To the very next martyr who sheds his blood for the Church. Who knows, your Grace, but that your enemies in England may gain you that honor!"[1] When Thomas was murdered two years later, the shrine of Fourvière was dedicated to him. Shortly thereafter, the son of King Louis VII was miraculously cured through the intercession of St. Thomas and in thanksgiving the king made a pilgrimage to Fourvière.

Blessed Pothinus, who had been entrusted with the care of the Lyons diocese, was over ninety years of age and physically very weak. He could scarcely breathe because of chronic physical weakness, but was strengthened by spiritual enthusiasm because of his pressing desire for martyrdom. . . . He was conveyed to the (Roman) tribunal by the soldiers, accompanied by the civil authorities and the whole populace, who shouted and jeered at him as though he were Christ Himself. But he bore noble witness. When the governor asked him, 'Who is the Christian's god?' He replied, 'If you are a fit person, you shall know.' Thereupon he was mercilessly dragged along beneath a rain of blows. . . . He was flung into prison, and two days later he passed away.
—Eusebius (d. 339)
The History of the Church from Christ to Constantine

St. Irenaeus is considered the first great Catholic theologian. He was born around 130 AD in what is now Turkey and became Bishop of Lyons around 178 AD. He is not mentioned after 190 but St. Gregory, Bishop of Tours, states in his *History of the Franks* that he was martyred though this is not certain. Irenaeus is famous for his work *Against Heresies* that was written to refute the heresy of Gnosticism, whose believers denied the divinity of Christ and the authority of the Gospels.

Irenaeus' writings are valuable because they highlight the importance of tradition in guiding the Church. In particular, he emphasized the special role of the Church in Rome, founded by Peter and Paul, which "because of its superior origin, all Churches must agree, that is, all the faithful in the whole world; and it is in her that the faithful everywhere have maintained the apostolic tradition."

Irenaeus also emphasized the early Christian belief in the Eucharist. "For as the bread of the earth, receiving the invocation of God, is no longer common bread but the Eucharist, consisting of two elements, earthly and heavenly, so also our bodies, when they receive the Eucharist, are no longer corruptible but have the hope of the resurrection into eternity."[2]

Pilgrims came to Fourvière through the centuries believing that Our Lady protected them from famine, plagues and pillaging. In 1643, the whole city was dedicated to Our Lady of Fourvière to stop an epidemic that was ravaging the city. During the French Revolution, terrible acts of sacrilege were carried out. An ass trampled on a crucifix and was

A woman closely associated with Fourvière is Pauline Jaricot, the foundress of The Society for the Propagation of the Faith, who was born in Lyons in 1799. In 1816, after listening to a sermon on vanity at the church of St. Nizier, Pauline, who loved fine clothes and flattery, totally changed her life. In the chapel at Fourvière on Christmas Eve, she offered her life to God.

One day she heard about the lack of funds available for the missions in the Far East and developed the idea of asking ten close associates to give a few cents a week to the missions. They in turn would ask ten of their own associates to do the same and so on. By 1910, the Society had raised millions of dollars in this simple way. One day, while in prayer, she had a vision of two lamps; one empty symbolizing Europe and one full of oil representing the people in mission countries. She understood this to mean that if France helped the work of the missions, their lamp might be refilled with the zeal of their old faith.

One of her endeavors resulted in bankruptcy, through no fault of her own, and the loss of her reputation. Pope Paul VI said, "More than others, Pauline had to encounter, accept, and overcome with love a number of objections, defeats, humiliations, and renunciations which would give her work the mark of the Cross and its mysterious productiveness." Pope John Paul II called her "a true disciple of Christ."[3] In 1930, the cause for her canonization was opened.

Ven. Pauline Jaricot

forced to drink out of a chalice. Pilgrims still came, visiting the shrine at night. The shrine was personally reopened by Pope Pius VII in 1805.

During the Napoleonic era, the shrine was spared destruction and the city escaped a subsequent outbreak of cholera. During the Commune massacres of 1830 and 1848, Lyons suffered less than most. One revolutionary exclaimed, "We shall never succeed as long as that montagnarde (mountain lady) is up there!"[4]

In 1851, St. Peter Julian Eymard received here what he called the "grace of Fourvière" when he realized that Jesus in the Blessed Sacrament "had no religious body to watch with Him, to honor Him, to procure His glory! Why not found something?"[5] Peter left his order and founded the Congregation of the Blessed Sacrament. St. John Vianney once brought his whole parish to the shrine.

In 1870, France was invaded by Prussia. The Catholics of Lyons vowed to build a church dedicated to the Blessed Virgin Mary if the siege were lifted. When their prayers were answered, they built a new basilica in thanksgiving for her intercession. It was consecrated in 1896. Inside, six large mosaics illustrate important events in the history of Christian France and the life of Mary as well as the honors given to her by the Church.

Pope John Paul II recognized the importance of Lyons when he visited the city in 1986 saying, "The Church, too, has always considered Lyons as a chosen portion, since the day when the first martyrs confessed their faith in the city where the first Bishop of the Gauls carried out his service."[6]

O Lady of Fourvière,
the people of Lyons turned to you during their hour of need,
and we too turn to you.
We ask you to protect our city, our home and our nation.
May your Son, Jesus, inspire in us a love for you
and a desire to emulate your care for His people. Amen.

Hail Holy Queen

Salve Regina

(King Louis VII requested that a daily Mass followed by the Salve Regina *be held in perpetuity at Fourvière)*

Hail! Holy Queen, Mother of mercy,
   our life, our sweetness and our hope.
To thee do we cry, poor banished children of Eve;
To thee do we send up our sighs, mourning and weeping
   in this vale of tears.
Turn then, O most gracious advocate,
   thine eyes of mercy towards us.
And after this our exile,
   show unto us the blessed fruit of thy womb, Jesus.
O clement! O loving! O sweet Virgin Mary!

Pray for us, O holy mother of God,
   that we may be made worthy of the promises of Christ.
Amen.

✤ *Three* ✤

Mont Saint-Michel

S t. Michael the Archangel has traditionally been known as the guardian angel of the people of God and protector of the Catholic Church. He is often depicted in art with a shield, sword and crown; symbols of his power over evil. His name, which means *Quis et Deus* ("Who is like unto God"), is in contrast to the fallen angels who wanted to be like God.

> *At that time there shall arise Michael. The great prince, guardian of your people.*
> —Daniel 12:1

According to the Book of Revelation, "War broke out in heaven; Michael and his angels battled against the dragon. The dragon and his angels fought back, but they did not prevail and there was no longer any place for them in heaven. The huge dragon, the ancient serpent, who is called the Devil and Satan, who deceived the whole world, was thrown down to earth, and its angels were thrown down with it" (Rev 12:7-9). The ancient serpent was the one who tricked Eve into eating from the tree of the knowledge of good and evil in Genesis 3.

St. Michael, the heavenly warrior, is credited with assisting men and women during many decisive moments in Church history. Constantine and Justinian built churches in honor of St. Michael's assistance. Charlemagne dedicated his kingdom to St. Michael. St. Michael appeared to Joan of Arc and told her to help the King of France. Pope Leo XIII (d. 1903) issued a prayer to St. Michael asking him to protect the Church from the

Mont Saint-Michel

devil. The Church celebrates the feast of the Archangels, Michael, Gabriel and Raphael, on September 29, also known as Michaelmas Day.

In his classic book *Mont Saint-Michel and Chartres*, Henry Adams (d. 1918), American historian and author, said that Michael is "the conqueror of Satan, the mightiest of all created spirits, the nearest to God. His place was where danger was greatest. . . . The Normans (Vikings who settled in northwest France), when they converted to Christianity, put themselves under his powerful protection. . . . So soldiers, nobles, and monarchs went on pilgrimage to his shrine; so the common people followed, and still follow, like ourselves."[1]

It has been revealed to various saints that the great Archangel is the special guardian of the Blessed Sacrament; that he accompanies It everywhere—in the hands of the priest, upon the throne of exposition, in the tabernacle, when borne in procession, on Its obscure visits to the sick, or wherever the love of the divine Victim may cause It to be borne. Day and night he keeps faithful vigil before the tabernacle in loving adoration.

—'Neath St. Michael's Shield

During the eighth century, St. Michael appeared in a dream to St. Aubert, the Bishop of Avranches, and requested that a church be built on Mont Saint-Michel. After Aubert obtained a relic of St. Michael from Monte Sant' Angelo in Italy, where the archangel had appeared in the fifth century, it became a favorite pilgrimage site. Prior to this, Mont Saint-Michel was known as Mount-Tombe where, according to Celtic tradition, it was a refuge for dead souls.

St. Aubert built the first oratory on the mount. It was followed by an abbey that adopted the Benedictine rule in the tenth century. The mount once stood within a forest but now it is surrounded by sands and sea. The tidal changes here are extreme, second only in the world to the Bay of Fundy in Newfoundland. At high tide, it was once accessible only by boat but now a causeway provides safe travel for pilgrims. It appears to be impregnable and no army has ever conquered it.

Mont Saint-Michel became a place where pilgrims experienced miraculous cures and the mighty came to ask for St. Michael's protection. On one occasion, an entire village suddenly left for the mount "forcing their parish priest to go with them and say Mass there."[2] King Louis XI established the Order of the Knights of St. Michael whose members wore a necklace of golden shells (pilgrims traditionally stitched shells on their clothing) upon which hung a medal of St. Michael slaying the dragon.

Veneration of St. Michael is the greatest remedy against despising the rights of God, against insubordination, skepticism and infidelity.[3]

—St. Francis de Sales

One victim of World War II, whose story was made known to the world by the movie *Au Revoir les Enfants* by Louis Malle, is Père Jacques Bunel, OCD. Père Jacques was born in 1900 and ordained a priest in 1925, joining the Carmelite Order in 1931. He was imprisoned briefly by the Germans in 1940 and, after his release, hid Jewish children in his school at Avon near Paris. In 1944, he was arrested and ultimately sent to Mauthausen concentration camp. A fellow prisoner said, "His presence was proof of the living God and, thanks to him, on Easter Day I had the overwhelming joy of receiving the Holy Eucharist from his hands, hiding behind a muddy block. He risked his life to do this."[4] His time in Mauthausen ruined his health and he died in 1945 shortly after the camp was liberated and was buried in Avon.

Père Jacques wrote, "The Word Incarnate is always there for us in the Eucharist. This overpowering mystery allows the unworthy hands of the priest to hold the same Body of Christ that the Virgin Mary held in her arms and pressed to her heart. It is the same Christ! The priest takes Christ in his hands and gives Him to others! When you receive Him, you are like the Virgin Mary during the months when she carried her child. You truly carry Christ within you."[5] Père Jacques was awarded the Medal of the Just by Israel in 1985. His cause has been opened for canonization.

Père Jacques
Bunel

After the French Revolution, Mont Saint-Michel was turned into a prison. In 1856, the relics of St. Aubert were moved to the Basilica of St. Gervais in nearby Avranches. In 1966, Benedictines returned to the mount. The golden statue of St. Michael on top of the Abbey still guards the people of God. It is a reminder that the battle we truly fight is not against earthly enemies, it is a war of good versus evil and the battle is for our soul.

St. Michael is the Patron Saint of Battle, and so it is very fitting that the cemeteries holding the remains of soldiers who died after the June 1944 D-Day landings should lie just northeast of Mont Saint-Michel. The American National Cemetery and Memorial at St. Laurent-sur-mer contains 9286 tombstones, of which 307 are unknown and bear the inscription, "Here rests in honoured glory a comrade in arms known but to God."

One beautiful memorial is in the Church at Ste. Mère-Église where a stained glass window depicts Mary hovering above the parachutists who landed in the middle of town during the airborne landings of June 6, 1944. On the outside of the church hangs a replica of a parachutist who got caught on the steeple during the night of the invasion.

The beauty and majesty of Mont Saint-Michel is best summed up by Henry Adams who said that the mount expresses "the unity of Church and State, God and Man, Peace and War, Life and Death, Good and Bad. . . . One looks back on it all as a picture; a symbol of unity; an assertion of God and Man in a bolder, stronger, closer union than ever was expressed by other art; and when the idea is absorbed, accepted, and perhaps partially understood, one may move on."[6]

O St. Michael,
we try to walk in the path illuminated for us by the Lord,
yet we falter;
We try to be brave, yet we lack courage.
Help us to know that the whole army of the heavenly hosts
is with us as we struggle to proclaim in word and deed
the truths of the Gospel.
Help us to know that Jesus Christ is King and Ruler of all the world
and our weakness is strengthened by Him. Amen.

Prayer to St. Michael
(Issued by Pope St. Leo XIII)

St. Michael the Archangel,
   Defend us in battle;
Be our protection
   against the wickedness and snares of the devil.
May God rebuke him, we humbly pray,
      and do thou, O Prince of the Heavenly Host,
      by the Divine power of God,
      cast into hell, Satan, and all the evil spirits
      who roam through the world
      seeking the ruin of souls. Amen.

✤ *Four* ✤

Bernard of Clairvaux

S t. Bernard of Clairvaux was probably the most influential man of the twelfth century. History books cite his impact on world events and the Church recognizes him as a Doctor of the Church, a man whose life and writings transcend his time. Drawn to solitude, he was reluctantly called upon to quell the great controversies of his day, acting on behalf of popes, emperors and bishops. In recognition of his eloquence, the Church calls him *Doctor Mellifluus*, the Honey-Sweet Doctor, as well as the last Western Father of the Church, for his philosophy was in the spirit of the early Church Fathers.

Bernard was born into a noble family at Fontaines-les-Dijon in Burgundy in 1090. He was the third oldest of seven children; six boys and one girl. His mother, Aleth, offered him to God at birth and, according to legend, dreamed that he would "one day guard the house of the Lord." One Christmas Eve, when he was a young boy, he too had a dream where he saw the child Jesus "as if just born of His Virgin Mother."[1] Throughout his life, Bernard had a special devotion to Mary and tradition attributes the words of the *Memorarae* to him as well as the last words of the *Salve Regina: O clement, O loving, O sweet Virgin Mary!*

> *The posthumous influence of the Abbot of Clairvaux was felt in the movement which little by little led the bishops and the Councils of the Church to prescribe for the faithful, about the close of the twelfth century, the recitation . . . of the greeting addressed by the Archangel Gabriel to the Virgin Mary, "Hail Mary, full of grace, the Lord is with thee, blessed art thou among women," and in addition the words of welcome spoken by Elizabeth, "Blessed is the fruit of thy womb." One finds the teaching of this prayer for the first time in Paris during 1198, and Orléans followed suit about the same time. Enriched finally with the words added by the Church, this became our* Ave Maria.[2]

—Georges Goyau

When Bernard was a teenager, his mother died. She was very involved in the spiritual life of the family and her loss was keenly felt. Bernard was a passionate man about all things and "realized that for ardent natures like his there are but two ways: the glories and delights of the world, or utter surrender to God."[3] He chose God. And he chose the life led by the monks of Citeaux, a poor and austere Benedictine monastery south of Dijon. Unlike Cluny, which was famous for its wealth and influence, Citeaux embraced the traditional rule of St. Benedict based on silence, obedience and humility. This was

St. Bernard

perfect for Bernard who said, "I was conscious that my weak character needed strong medicine."[4]

Bernard was expected to pursue a brilliant career but he convinced his uncle and four of his brothers to follow him to Citeaux. Their father, Tescelin, blessed their departure, asking only that his son try to contain some of his zeal. When Bernard and his entourage finally reached Citeaux, which hadn't had a new vocation in several years, there were thirty men with him! He had such a compelling personality that mothers hid their sons when he passed by their homes lest they join him too. Even his father and youngest brother joined him later on.

At Citeaux, he had hopes of "dying there to the hearts and minds of men,"[5] but his superior, St. Stephen Harding, quickly recognized his leadership capabilities. When he was only twenty-five, he was made abbot of a new house in the Valley of Light or Clairvaux. In the midst of hunger, poverty and cold, Bernard and his fellow monks raised up the famous abbey of Clairvaux. Even though Bernard was physically frail, he did not avoid hard labor or severe penances. He suffered from ill health as a result.

Bernard preferred Clairvaux but he was obliged to leave his monastery as his renown as a man of wisdom spread. His influence extended to popes as well as kings and he spoke to them not as a subject but as a spiritual advisor. Speaking frankly to Emperor Lothair, who had mistakenly treated the people of Pisa badly, he wrote, "I wonder at whose instigation or advice you allowed yourself to be so hoodwinked."[6] Yet Bernard, as the Trappist monk Thomas Merton said, "could be as tender as a mother to anyone who did not give evidence of being a hardened pharisee, and who had in his heart something of Christ's unending patience with the weak sinner."[7]

Given Bernard's reputation, it was inevitable that he would be called upon to resolve the crises that embroiled the Church. In 1130, when both Innocent II and Anacletus II claimed to be Pope, King Louis VI convened the Council of Étampes to decide the issue for France. Bernard was asked to judge the

Besides Clairvaux, three abbeys figured prominently in Bernard's life: Cluny, Fontenay and Vézelay.

Cluny, its remnants still an impressive sight, was the greatest and most influential monastery in France. It was founded in 910 and quickly became a center of learning and influence. Following the rule of St. Benedict, as its wealth increased, its austerity decreased. The monks were in decline by the French Revolution (eighteenth century) and most of Cluny was destroyed, but what is left show us the grandeur of what was described as "a place for angels to dwell should they come down to earth."[8]

Fontenay was especially close to Bernard's heart for it was built near his childhood home. It is the best preserved example of Bernard's style of monastic architecture. Founded in 1118 by Bernard himself, it was called Fontenay because it was surrounded by springs and brooks. It is now in private hands and beautifully restored.

Vézelay gained renown as the purported site of St. Mary Magdalene's relics. It was a starting point for pilgrims on the road to Santiago de Compostela and the site where, in 1146, Bernard preached the Second Crusade whose failure was a great disappointment to him. Approaching Vézelay from afar, pilgrims used to cry out "Montjoie!" (Mount of Joy). It can still be seen as Bernard would have seen it, high on a hill, an earthly Jerusalem.

Cluny

merits of the two, deciding in favor of Innocent II. From then on, he worked tirelessly to end the schism. When he met with King Henry I of England, who worried about making the wrong decision, Bernard told him, "Worry about the other sins for which you will be answerable to God. As for this one, I take it upon myself!"[9] Traveling throughout Europe, he won over the influential leaders and bishops of Europe and, when Anacletus died, his successor ended the schism.

A holdout towards ending the schism was the Bishop of Angoulême along with his ally, William, Count of Poitiers. Bernard, unsuccessful in reasoning with William, invited him to attend a Mass. In anticipation of a showdown, the church was packed. Since William had been excommunicated, he stood at the back of the church. At communion time, Bernard processed to the back of the church carrying a consecrated host and faced William. "We have petitioned you and you have ignored us; we have sat at your feet in council, and you have disdained us. Now behold the Virgin's Son, the head of the Church you persecute; behold your judge before whom the heavens bow down. Do you despise him? Are you going to treat Him in the same way that you treat His servants?"[10] William collapsed at these words, reconciled with the Bishop of Poitiers and ultimately founded two daughter houses of Clairvaux before dying on a pilgrimage to Spain.

One of the most famous episodes involving Bernard was his confrontation with Peter Abelard, who is well known today for his love affair with Heloise. Abelard was a popular theologian and philosopher but, as Theodore Ratisbonne said in his book on Bernard, "his inexcusable fault was the application of the principles of free examination to dogmatic truths."[11] Abelard espoused faith through reason. Bernard held the traditional view that the mysteries of faith are beyond human reason. Ready to defend his views, Abelard requested a hearing at the Council of Sens. Bernard reluctantly agreed to represent the Church and spoke so eloquently that Abelard was speechless. Abelard retired to Cluny where he consecrated his remaining days to God. Peter the Venerable, the Abbot of Cluny, said, "Death, the bearer of good tidings, found him—not like so many asleep, but awake."[12]

In modern times, Bernard is sometimes accused of coming down hard on people whom he regarded as enemies of the Church. In his book on neglected saints, Edward Watkin wrote, "This Bernard of flesh and blood with his human defects and faults but aflame with love for God and for his Church is more vital, more credible, less remote, a more persuasive apostle of holiness than the faultless plaster-of-Paris saint which a conventional devotion would set in his place."[13]

> *The means and appliances for this vast and sustained superiority of the individual over his age were all contained within the four walls of his cell; or, more truly, within the one great heart, inflamed with the love of God; the solitary intelligence, illuminated by the light of faith; and the single will, energetic in itself, and made inflexible by union with the Divine.*[14]
>
> —Cardinal Henry Manning

Bernard's influence on the world stemmed from his intimate relationship with God. He mixed the contemplative life with the active life saying that prayer kept the two in balance. A person can be "deemed perfect in whose soul these three harmoniously meet: He who knows how to sigh for himself, to exult in God, and to assist his neighbor in his needs."[15] His reflections on the Song of Songs are considered classical mystical writing. Bernard was "never more filled with sweetness than when he expounded (on) the great love-poem of the Bridegroom and the Bride, Christ and the Church, the Divine Word and the soul."[16] Still read today is Bernard's work *De Consideratione* which he wrote for Pope Eugene III (d. 1153) but was also bedside reading for Pope John XXIII.

> *There is a place where God is perceived, truly resting and restful, the place not of Judge, nor of the Master, but of the Spouse. O place of true quietude, which not without reason, I think, is called the bedchamber. . . . That version terrifies not, it soothes; it excites no restless curiosity, but it calms; nor does it fatigue the*

senses, but tranquilizes. Here is true rest. The tranquil God tranquilizes all things, and to behold Him is to rest.[17]

—St. Bernard

Even though Bernard was absent for long periods of time, Clairvaux flourished. By the time he died, seven hundred monks lived at Clairvaux. During his lifetime, sixty-eight monasteries were founded by him. Two of the most famous were Fontenay and, due to his friendship with St. Malachy, Mellifont in Ireland. Malachy died at Clairvaux in 1148. In failing health, Bernard spent the last years of his life not in solitude but wherever the Church needed him. He said, "The spirit is ready in an infirm flesh."[18]

Once God is found, the soul has rest; for just as on this side no rest recalls, so beyond the grave no unrest ever troubles any more.[19]

—St. Bernard

Bernard died in 1153 at Clairvaux. For a man who wanted to unite his soul to God in prayerful solitude, Bernard enjoyed a fame not known by many. His gifts, which could have remained hidden in a monastery, were humbly used to further the work of the Church. He was proclaimed a saint in 1174 and a Doctor of the Church by Pope Pius VIII in 1830.

Though Clairvaux is gone, the Cistercians remain, divided into two branches: the Common Observance and the Cistercian Order of the Strict Observance or Trappists. Thomas Merton from Gethsemani Abbey in Kentucky is the most famous Trappist of modern times.

O Bernard,
you totally gave your life to God,
and even though you desired solitude
you were obedient to God's call to serve his people.
Help me to understand that what I may desire
and what God asks of me may be different.
Like you, I ask for the grace and humility to be obedient to God's call.
Lord, I give all that I have to you;
I desire to serve only you. Amen.

Psalm 118:5-9

*(Before Bernard confronted Abelard at the Council of Sens,
he prayed this Psalm)*

In danger I called on the LORD;
> The LORD answered me and set me free.
The LORD is with me; I am not afraid;
> what can mortals do against me?
The LORD is with me as my helper;
> I shall look in triumph on my foes.
Better to take refuge in the LORD
> than to put one's trust in mortals.
Better to take refuge in the LORD
> than to put one's trust in princes.

✤ *Five* ✤
Notre-Dame

If one could pick a focal point in Christian France from which all else radiated, it would be the cathedral of Our Lady—Notre-Dame. It would be appropriate, too, because from this place in France, all road distances are measured. The cathedral was once prominent in a small city; now it is engulfed in a huge city but it is still the center of Catholic life in Paris.

Hilaire Belloc (d. 1953), the Catholic historian and writer, described Notre-Dame as "a lady grown old in a great house, about whose age new phrases and strange habits have arisen, who is surrounded by youth of her own lineage, and yet is content to hear and understand without replying to their speech. She is silent in the midst of energy, and forgotten in the many activities of the household, yet she is the center of the estate."[1]

The basilica of St. Denis was the traditional burial site for royalty and Reims Cathedral the coronation site, but historic events always seemed to involve the great cathedral, perhaps because in times of trial or great joy, our thoughts turn to God and no other place captures the spiritual heart of Paris like Notre-Dame. Pope John Paul II said, "This is an historical place, a sacred place."[2]

Notre-Dame

Notre-Dame resides, along with the Sainte-Chapelle, on Île de la Cité, an island in the Seine River where the Parisii, a Gallic tribe, settled in the third century BC. The city, originally named Lutetia, eventually became known as Paris in recognition of the original inhabitants. Paris was conquered by the Romans in 52 BC and Christianity was introduced by St. Denis in 250 AD.

Originally, the Île de la Cité contained a temple to Jupiter. In the sixth century, Childebert I built the Cathedral Church of Saint-Étienne, the foundation of which rests under Notre-Dame today.

Construction of the present cathedral began in the twelfth century. It became the site of great ceremonial occasions such as the coronation of Henry VI of England, the coronation of Mary Queen of Scots and the coronation of Napoleon and Josephine attended by Pope Pius VII (a huge painting of the event by Jacques Louis David [d. 1825] can be seen in the Louvre). The Church's hymn of thanksgiving, the *Te Deum*, was sung here following Henry IV's conversion to Catholicism and after the Allied victory over Germany in 1918. Charles de Gaulle joined in the singing of the *Magnificat* in the cathedral amidst gunfire after his triumphant entry into Paris in 1944 and a requiem Mass was held for him here in 1970. Pope John Paul II beatified Frederic Ozanam, the founder of the St. Vincent de Paul society, during a Mass at Notre-Dame in 1997.

> *Notre-Dame is vast: it is not gigantic. Its pillars are powerful: they are not massive. Its vault rises high, but not oppressive. Here lies the first miracle of Notre-Dame: harmony, equilibrium, proportion. The cathedral is the house of God and man. Man is elevated here but God does not crush him. The genius of the architects was to have expressed Christian faith with such accuracy.*[3]
>
> —Jacques Perrier, Bishop of Chartres

During the French Revolution, much of the statuary of the cathedral was destroyed, bells were melted down and the cathedral became a "Temple of Reason." Viollet-le-Duc conducted a restoration in the mid-nineteenth century. Some of the original statues are in the Cluny Museum while King David's head can be seen in the Metropolitan Museum of Art in New York. What remains today is a Gothic masterpiece,

The patron saint of Paris is St. Geneviève, a consecrated woman from Nanterre, who was born about 422. When she was a young girl, her piety was noticed by St. Germain, the Bishop of Auxerre, who blessed her desire to be a spouse of Jesus. Geneviève persuaded the Parisians to fast and pray when Atilla the Hun threatened the city, correctly predicting that they would be saved if they did so. After the Franks besieged Paris, Geneviève was able to bring in food to alleviate the famine.

After her death, the people of Paris still sought her help when danger loomed. In 1129, an epidemic ceased after her relics were carried in procession. During World War I, the faithful of Paris again asked for her intercession as the Germans marched towards Paris. The Germans turned back. During World War II, the people did not process with her relics and the Germans invaded Paris. Robert Gordon Anderson in his book *The Biography of a Cathedral* notes, "perhaps that was the trouble—or the failure to do so was symbolic of the trouble."

Geneviève was buried next to King Clovis and his wife St. Clotilda. Her remains were exhumed and burnt during the Revolution but her sarcophagus and a few relics were brought to the Church of St. Étienne-du-Mont. Inside the Panthéon are paintings of her life by Puvis de Chavannes, including the one on the cover of this book of St. Geneviève blessing the city of Paris.

Notre-Dame, given its place of prominence in the city, would seem to be the likely burial place for the kings of France. But with the exception of Clovis, the early kings were buried at St-Germain-des-Prés while the later kings were interred on the outskirts of Paris at the Basilica of St-Denis. According to tradition, Denis, the first Bishop of Paris, was decapitated at Montmartre and carried his own head to the area of the present basilica. A church dedicated to St. Denis was probably begun by St. Geneviève c. 475 but the church seen today dates from the eleventh and twelfth centuries. For 1200 years, most of the kings of France were buried at St-Denis including Louis XVI and his queen, Marie Antoinette. During the Revolution, the graves were opened and the remains thrown into a communal grave. In 1816, some of the tombs were returned empty to the basilica.

St. Denis

different in appeal from its elegant neighbor the Sainte-Chapelle but glorious in its strength and splendor.

The main doorway of Notre-Dame, facing the parvis or plaza, illustrates in sculpture the Last Judgment and is flanked by the Portal to the Virgin and the Portal to St. Anne. Above the doorways are twenty-eight statues of the kings of Judah and Israel who preceded Christ, restored by Viollet-le-Duc after they were destroyed during the Revolution because the mobs mistakenly thought that they represented the kings of France.

Notre-Dame has always had a mysterious power over human destiny. It persuaded Gandhi that "the men who made such things must have had the love of God in their hearts. . . ." And even Saint-Simon (d. 1752), most worldly of diarists, felt constrained to write down the story of Chardon, the great lawyer and his wife, who were convinced Huguenots until they were kept waiting in their carriage one morning on the Parvis de Notre-Dame. "Madame Chardon was looking idly about her," Saint-Simon tells us, "when her eyes happened to fall on the west door of Notre-Dame. Little by little she fell into a deep reverie—or perhaps it would be more accurate to say 'a profound meditation.' Finally her husband noticed this, and asked what was the matter, and nudged her with his elbow to make her answer. And she said that as the statues of the saints had been on the west door of Notre-Dame for centuries before Luther or Calvin were born, this showed that the people had been praying to the saints for many centuries, and that the reformers ideas were relatively new . . . when one compared them with the ancient traditions of Catholicism; and although she had never thought of this before, it was causing her grave disquiet." Both Chardons retired from the world and returned to it as convinced Catholics.

—John Russell
Paris

Inside the cathedral, all eyes rise to the great rose windows. In the north window, containing mostly thirteenth century glass, the Virgin Mary is surrounded by Old Testament figures. In the south rose window, Christ is surrounded by angels, saints and martyrs. Near the high altar is a statue of King Louis XIII who consecrated France to the Blessed Virgin Mary.

The treasury houses the Crown of Thorns, the Holy Nail and a piece of the True Cross which are displayed on Good Friday. Previously these relics, acquired by St. Louis, were in the Sainte-Chapelle. A walk up the south tower will provide those with strong legs a beautiful view of the city.

Paul Claudel, the French poet and writer, wrote about his conversion which took place in Notre-Dame on Christmas Day, 1886, during a Mass. "The choir boys . . . were just about to sing that which I learned later to be the *Magnificat* . . . . And it was then that (I had an experience) which dominates all of my life. In an instant my heart was touched and I believed. I believed with such a clinging force, such a lifting up of my being, with so powerful a conviction, with such a certitude void of any kind of doubt, that since that time, not all the books, nor all the reasonings, nor all the vicissitudes of an agitated life, have been able to shake my faith, nor indeed touch it. I had, all of the sudden, a heart-rending sense of innocence, of the eternal infancy of God, an unspeakable revelation."[4]

In the midst of revolution, two world wars and the destruction of the monarchy, Notre-Dame remains, a reminder to us that all those who place themselves under Our Lady's protection are not lost. A monstrance in the treasury illustrates this; it shows Our Lady in the symbolic ship of the city of Paris, our sure refuge in any storm.

Notre-Dame, Our Lady,
we appeal to you today to protect our country
as you have protected France throughout the ages.
May the poor, the forgotten, the unborn, and the sick
know of your Motherly concern and care.
Help us to live our lives as you did;
with selfless concern for others and total trust in your Son. Amen.

Te Deum

(According to tradition, the Te Deum *was first sung after St. Augustine's baptism though many now believe that the ancient hymn was composed by St. Nicetus [d. 414])*

You are God: we praise you;
You are Lord: we acclaim you;
You are eternal Father:
All creation worships you.

To you all angels, all the powers of heaven
Cherubim and Seraphim, sing in endless praise:
    Holy, holy, holy, Lord. God of power and might,
    heaven and earth are full of your glory.

The glorious company of apostles praise you.
The noble fellowship of the prophets praise you.
The white-robed martyrs praise you.

Throughout the world the holy Church acclaims you:
    Father, of majesty unbounded,
    your true and only Son, worthy of all worship,
    and the Holy Spirit, advocate and guide.

You, Christ, are the king of glory,
    the eternal Son of the Father.

When you became man to set us free
    you did not spurn the Virgin's womb.

You overcame the sting of death,
    and opened the kingdom of heaven to all believers.

You are seated at God's right hand in glory.
We believe that you will come and be our judge.
Come then, Lord, and help your people,
    bought with the price of your own blood,
    and bring us with your saints
    to glory everlasting.

✠ *Six* ✠

King Louis IX

It is unusual to find a king cited as a great saint, but St. Louis was regarded as one during his lifetime and declared a saint by the Church after his death. Joinville, his biographer, wrote, "Most sainted monarchs were deficient in either piety or statesmanship. . . . The perfect Christian king was an ideal never to be realized until Christ the King Himself reigned on earth, but mortal monarchs were nonetheless dutybound to strive to rule with justice because they were kings and with piety because they were Christians. To the confusion and admiration of his contemporaries, none came closer to attaining this difficult ideal than St. Louis."[1]

Louis was born in 1214 at Poissy, a town a few miles west of Paris on the Seine River. He was baptized shortly thereafter, an event, he said, that was "a greater gift and incomparable dignity above all honors and earthly rewards."[2] His baptismal font can still be seen in the church of Notre-Dame. He became king of France in 1226 after the sudden death of his father, Louis VIII. His mother, Blanche of Castile, was named Regent and was described as "the Queen who made peace and kept peace and, by her unaided genius, preserved the crown of France for her son."[3]

St. Louis

In 1234, Louis married Margaret of Provence, a union that produced eleven children. Blanche was jealous of Margaret and tried to minimize the time her son and daughter-in-law spent together. According to Joinville, the king's attendants used to warn him of his mother's approach so he could slip away from Margaret's presence to his own room.

What differentiated Louis from other rulers was that he "brought to Capetian royalty a moral authority which it was never to find again."[4] Joinville said, "Twenty-two years was I with him; and I never heard him swear by God or His mother or His saints. When he wished to be emphatic, he used to say, 'In truth it was so' or 'In truth it is so.'"[5] A woman once mocked his adherence to the Church and told him that he was not fit to be king. Louis responded, "You surely speak true—I am unworthy to be king, but if it had pleased Our Lord, another who knew better how to govern would be in my place."[6]

Louis viewed his kingship as inseparable from his duty to be a good Christian. A biographer once said of Louis, "The saints made their perfection consist in the exact fulfillment of their duty. St. Louis was a great king because he strove to be a great saint. He became a great saint because he strove to be a good king."[7]

I ask that supplications, prayers, petitions and thanksgivings be offered for everyone, for kings and all in authority, that we might lead a quiet and tranquil life in all devotion and dignity. This is good and pleasing to God our savior, who wills everyone to be saved and to come to knowledge of the truth.
—1 Timothy 2:1-4

Louis attended Mass two or more times a day and when people complained that this was time-consuming, he said, "If I spent twice that time in amusements, like hunting, no one would have any objection." Louis knelt during Mass and when he was offered a kneeler he said, "At Mass, God offers Himself as a sacrifice, and when God sacrifices Himself, kings should kneel on the floor."[8]

Louis was noted for his many charitable endeavors and for his reform of government. He helped to fund the institute that later became known as the Sorbonne and built the hospital of Quinze-Vingts for blind men. He regularly fed the poor—sometimes by his own hands and at his

The Sainte-Chapelle or the Holy Chapel is a masterpiece of Gothic architecture on the Île de la Cité in Paris. Built by St. Louis, it has been called "one of the most beautiful mansions of paradise."[9] Like Chartres Cathedral, the windows are its treasure but it was originally built to house another treasure, the Crown of Thorns. St. Louis purchased the Crown of Thorns from the Latin emperor of Constantinople. The king later acquired a piece of the True Cross and fragments of other relics.

To provide these holy relics with a suitable resting place, Louis commissioned the building of a new chapel attached to the royal palace. It contained an upper chapel dedicated to the Holy Crown and the Holy Cross while the lower chapel was dedicated to Mary. On Good Friday, the sick were permitted to touch the relics. After St. Louis' death, a reliquary containing his head was added to the chapel.

The Sainte-Chapelle was badly damaged during the Revolution and the reliquaries were melted down. The chapel was restored in 1867 but is now a museum. During World Youth Day in 1997, the relics were brought back to the Sainte-Chapelle for one day of prayer. As Cardinal Francis George said, "It became a very holy place in the middle of that secular place."[10] For those who cannot travel to France to see the beautiful stained glass windows in person, a replica of the chapel can be seen in Chicago at the Quigley Preparatory Seminary.

own table. He organized the rules of law, developed a royal court of justice and had his officials swear to enforce the law fairly across all segments of society. On occasion, he used to sit under an oak tree in Vincennes to address any cases brought forward. Even King Henry III of England asked Louis to be an arbiter in a dispute with his nobles.

St. Louis was the man to reform Europe had Europe been capable of reform. This king caused France to be honored abroad and gave her an organized government. He was in all respects a model man. His piety was that of a hermit, but this did not detract from his kingly virtue. . . . Prudent and firm in the council chamber, brave but not rash on the battlefield, he was full of compassion as if he had never known anything but misfortune. Is it given to man to practice virtue in a higher degree?[11]
—Voltaire

During Louis' reign, Sts. Thomas Aquinas and Bonaventure, both Doctors of the Church, studied and taught in Paris. Bonaventure, who is considered the second founder of the Franciscans after St. Francis, preached one fifth of his homilies in front of the king. A famous story about Thomas and Louis illustrates the humility of the king. Thomas was seated next to Louis, who preferred that no business be conducted in the evening. Thomas, engrossed in his own thoughts, did not say a word to the king. Suddenly, Thomas brought his fist down on the table and said, "That settles the Manichees!"[12] (Manicheanism was an old heresy.) Louis, his pride not hurt at being ignored, quickly summoned his secretary to record Thomas' thoughts.

After Louis recovered from a serious illness in 1244, he vowed to go to the Holy Land to alleviate the plight of the Christians. Leaving his mother Blanche in charge, Louis, along with Margaret, embarked on a crusade in 1248 that took him away from home for almost six years. The crusaders captured the Egyptian city of Damietta, but within a year, his army surrendered to the Moslem Saracens and Louis was taken prisoner. After a ransom was paid, Louis was free but he returned home in 1254 a more sober man. Pope Boniface VIII said, "He did not live nor was clothed as before, although his life and conversation before were honest enough. For afterwards, the clothes he wore were religious not regal, not those of a knight but of a simple man."[13]

Never forgetting the suffering of the Christians, he left on another crusade in 1270 but died of the plague in Tunis, North Africa. He was buried in Saint-Denis, though some of his relics were given to other places like the Sainte-Chapelle. He was canonized in 1297.

Someone once told Louis about a Eucharistic miracle in which the host had turned into flesh and blood in the priest's hands. Louis said, "You, who are unbelievers, go and see this sight, for I firmly believe in all that the holy Church teaches us of the Sacrament of the Altar. And do you know what my reward will be for having in this mortal life believed exactly the teachings of the holy Church? I shall have in heaven a finer crown than the angels."[14]

O St. Louis,
we thank you for showing us how to live a Christian life
even in the midst of the world.
By your prayers, may we emulate your fidelity to Christ
in our families, our jobs, our world.
O Jesus, help of kings, guide and inspire me. Amen.

Psalm 5:1-9

(As he was dying, King Louis recited this Psalm)

Hear my words, O LORD;
listen to my sighing.
Hear my cry for help,
    my king, my God!
To you I pray, O LORD;
    at dawn you will hear my cry;
    at dawn I will plead before you and wait.

You are not a god who delights in evil;
    no wicked person finds refuge in you;
    the arrogant cannot stand before you.
You hate all who do evil;
    you destroy all who speak falsely.
Murderers and deceivers
    the LORD abhors.

But I can enter your house
    because of your great love.
I can worship in your holy temple
    because of my reverence for you, LORD.
Guide me in your justice because of my foes;
    make straight your way before me.

✤ *Seven* ✤

Chartres

Chartres, a small town dominated by its great cathedral, is located approximately sixty miles southwest of Paris. The cathedral, consecrated to the Assumption of the Blessed Virgin Mary in 1260, is well known for its beautiful stained glass windows and sculptures. It was the site of great medieval pilgrimages and was "thought of as the earthly palace of the Queen of Heaven."[1]

Chartres Cathedral was built in a relatively short period of time and, therefore, captures in a single place the beauty of Gothic architecture unaltered through the centuries. It was built on a Romanesque foundation; the crypt, towers and Royal Doorway are from the eleventh and twelfth centuries. But the rest of the cathedral is thirteenth century artistry at its best. Chartres Cathedral survived the destruction that afflicted many other church buildings during the French Revolution and the two World Wars.

Before Christianity came to Chartres, the people honored an unnamed virgin. With the advent of Christianity, this honor was transferred to the Virgin Mary, an action similar to the one mentioned by St. Paul who saw an inscription "to an unknown God" (Acts 17:23) and told the Athenian people, "What therefore you unknowingly worship, I proclaim to you." Chartres' popularity as a shrine to the Virgin Mary only increased when, in 876, Charles

Sancta Camisia (the Holy Veil)

the Bald, Charlemagne's grandson, gave the cathedral the *Sancta Camisia*, the Holy Veil or Tunic of the Blessed Virgin. Chartres, like Lourdes today, was known for the miraculous cures granted through Our Lady's intercession.

Catholic bishops were assigned to Chartres as early as the fourth century. An early church, on the site of the present cathedral, burned in 743 and another church was destroyed by the Vikings in 858. St. Fulbert, the Bishop of Chartres, rebuilt the cathedral after a fire in 1020, but most of it was destroyed by another fire in 1194. Miraculously, the *Sancta Camisia* survived and the people rallied together to rebuild once again. In 1260, the new cathedral was consecrated, built in a remarkably short period of time which accounts for its uniformity. The French Revolution caused little physical damage to the structure, but it was temporarily turned into a "Temple of Reason." In 1939, the stained glass windows were removed to a secure location before the Germans invaded France.

> *At last we are face to face with the crowning glory of Chartres. Other churches have glass—quantities of it and very fine—but we have been trying to catch a glimpse of the glory which stands behind the glass of Chartres, and gives it a quality and feeling of its own. For once the architect is useless and his explanations are pitiable; the painter helps still less; and the decorator, unless he works in glass, is the poorest guide of all. . . . You had better stop here, once for all, unless you are willing to feel that Chartres was made what it is, not by the artist but by the Virgin.*
> —Henry Adams
> *Mont Saint-Michel and Chartres*

The cathedral's prized possessions are the more than 160 stained glass windows that date mostly from the thirteenth century though some are older. Many have been restored and the beautiful colors and scenes can now be fully appreciated and used for instruction as they were originally intended. The Tree of Jesse at the west end of the nave wonderfully illustrates the vibrant colors while the Notre-Dame de la Belle Verriere

One of the early saints remembered at Chartres is St. Hilary of Poitiers (c. 315-367) who is called the Athanasius of the West because, like his forerunner, he defended the Church against the Arians who denied that Jesus was both God and man. Hilary was born in Poitiers and was a convert to Christianity. He was one of the most important early saints of France and his likeness can be seen in many ancient churches.

Hilary wrote, "We speak in an absurd and godless manner about the divinity of Christ's nature in us—the subject which we are discussing—unless we have learned it from Him. He Himself declares: 'For my flesh is food indeed, and my blood is drink indeed. He who eats my flesh and drinks my blood abides in me and I in him.' It is no longer permitted us to raise doubts about the true nature of the body and blood, for, according to the statement of the Lord Himself as well as our faith, this is indeed flesh and blood. And these things that we receive bring it about that we are in Christ and Christ in us."[2] Hilary of Poitiers was declared a Doctor of the Church by Pope Pius IX in 1851.

Just north of Poitiers, a decisive battle took place. At the Battle of Tours in 732, Charles Martel defeated the Moors of Spain and thus stopped the Moslem advances into France. As Hilaire Belloc, the French writer, said, "Thus was Christendom saved."[3]

Another saint honored at Chartres is St. Martin of Tours. Martin was born c. 316 in what is now Hungary. His family was pagan but he was drawn to the Catholic Church. According to legend, Martin was stationed in the army at Amiens when he encountered a beggar and cut his cloak in two to give half to the poor man. The Lord appeared to Martin in a dream wearing the halved cloak and said, "Martin, as yet but a catechumen, has clothed me with this garment." Martin was quickly baptized and left the army saying, "I am a soldier of Christ; it is not lawful for me to fight."[4]

St. Hilary ordained Martin as an exorcist and Martin established a monastery near Poitiers, the first of its kind in Gaul. He became a bishop by popular acclaim though some of his fellow bishops considered his unkempt appearance contemptible. Martin died in c. 397 in Candes and his burial site in Tours became a popular pilgrimage site. The ancient crypt, once containing the tomb of St. Martin, now lies beneath a modern basilica. Angelo Roncalli, later Pope John XXIII, had a great devotion to St. Martin and placed a plaque in the crypt in 1945 which read, "Blessed Martin preserve the clergy and people of Gaul. Look after your own everywhere."[5]

St. Martin of Tours

window, dating from the twelfth century, especially shows off the blue glass that is unique to the cathedral.

The sculptures are very lifelike and equally impressive. A prime example is the statue of Abraham cradling the head of his son Isaac at the central portal, north transept. This row of statues depict the Old Testament figures who prefigured Christ: Melchizedek, the first high priest, holding a chalice and censor; Abraham offering Isaac as a sacrifice to Yahweh; Moses holding the tablets of the Law and the staff of the seraph serpent; Samuel presenting the lamb to be slain; and David, King of the Israelites, holding a lance and the crown of thorns. The south doorway shows scenes from the Last Judgment. The devil can be seen escorting a miser and gossip into hell.

The book of the cathedral revealed to us sublime and familiar and tender things. I am thinking, for instance, of a sculptured group representing the creation of man. Christ is fashioning him with love, this first man, whose head, still vague, rests upon the knees of God. I can still see the beautiful, pensive face of "God creating the world."

—Raïssa Maritain
We Have Been Friends Together and
Adventures in Grace

Behind the cathedral, the chapel of St. Piat contains precious relics, most notably the *Sancta Camisia*. The visitor today is traveling in the footsteps of the many pilgrims who often walked hundreds of miles to see this holy relic. Some of the most famous pilgrims include Sts. Bernard, Louis de Montfort and Vincent de Paul. Organized pilgrimages still take place every year including one from Sacré-Coeur in Paris.

Charles Péguy, the French poet and essayist (1873-1914), is an example of a modern pilgrim. He wrote, "My (son) has been ill. . . . Well, old chap, I felt it was pretty serious. I had to make a vow, yes I did. I made a pilgrimage to Chartres. I am a Beauce man. Chartres is my cathedral. I was quite out of training. I did 144 kilometers in three days. . . . You see the spire of Chartres seventeen kilometers away across the plain. Occasionally, it disappears behind a fold in the ground or a line of wood. As soon as I saw it, it was absolute ec-

Chartres Cathedral

stasy. I stopped feeling, neither my tiredness nor my feet troubled me no more."[6] Charles died in 1914 during the World War I Battle of the Marne.

Warrren Carroll, the historian and founder of Christendom College, writes, "A day spent at Chartres Cathedral is worth a hundred books in making the climax of Christendom come alive."[7] Malcolm Miller wrote, "For the medieval pilgrim, drawn by the cathedral steeples, like beacons, beckoning from afar, the cathedral awaiting them at the end of their journey would similarly be a symbol for the heavenly Jerusalem awaiting his soul at the end of its journey."[8]

O Mary, Virgin honored at Chartres,
St. Bernard said that the
Son shall answer the prayers of the Mother
and the Father shall answer the prayers of the Son.
With this hope we turn to you,
and ask that you present our needs to your Son. Amen.

The Magnificat
(Spoken by Our Lady [Luke 1:46-55] and traditionally said in the evening)

My soul proclaims the greatness of the Lord,
my spirit rejoices in God my Savior
for he has looked with favor on his lowly servant.

From this day all generations will call me blessed:
the Almighty has done great things for me,
and holy is his Name.

He has mercy on those who fear him in every generation.

He has shone the strength of his arm,
he has scattered the proud in their conceit.

He has cast down the mighty from their thrones,
and has lifted up the lowly.

He has filled the hungry with good things,
and the rich he has sent away empty.

He has come to the help of his servant Israel
for he has remembered his promise of mercy,
the promise he made to our fathers,
to Abraham and his children forever.

✣ Eight ✣

Joan of Arc

Orléans is the site of one of the most significant battles ever fought in the history of the western world. At stake was the very survival of France. The inspiration behind this victory for France was not a general or a king but a teenage girl who took her orders from the "king of kings" (Rev 1:14). Her name was Joan of Arc.

France was in the midst of the Hundred Years War. Her enemies, the English, had won decisive victories on French soil, most notably at Crécy (1346) and Agincourt (1415). France itself was divided into two warring factions: those supporting the yet to be crowned French king, Charles VII, and the Burgundians who sided with the English. The young French king was an indecisive leader. His destiny was improbably placed in the young hands of Joan of Arc.

Joan was born in 1412 in Domrémy on the border between the provinces of Champagne and Lorraine. Her family name was d'Arc, but Joan always referred to herself as Jeanne-la-Pucelle or Joan the Maid. From all accounts, Joan was an ordinary girl who never learned to read or write. Nothing extraordinary was noted that could account for her sudden and brief appearance in history.

Joan first heard what she called "the voices" when she was about thirteen.

As she walked near a church, someone, whom she later identified as St. Michael the Archangel, called out her name. The voice said, "Jeanette, Jeanette, be good and wise; love God very much. Go to church often."[1] She took a vow of perpetual virginity and began to call herself Joan the Maid.

Joan heard the voices and saw visions for the rest of her life. Among those who communicated with her were Sts. Catherine of Alexandria and Margaret of Antioch. They asked her to live a life of holiness, pray regularly, receive Communion often and go to Confession. She did

St. Joan of Arc

not tell her family about these events. Eventually, she was told that she must leave home to embark upon a mission to liberate her beloved France! Joan was astonished for she was "only a poor girl" who couldn't even read or ride a horse. But the voices said, "Daughter of God, go, go, go. I will be your helper. Go!"[2]

Joan traveled to the local commander at Vaucouleurs, Robert de Baudricourt, who did not initially believe her. But eventually, in 1429, he provided her with an escort to meet with the king at Chinon. As a test, the king hid himself in a crowd but Joan immediately picked him out. She told him, "I am Joan the Maid, and the King of Heaven commands that through me you are to be anointed and crowned in the city of Reims as a lieutenant of the King of Heaven, who is king of France." Joan told Charles a secret known by him and God alone. A group of churchmen was called together to question her. They concluded that the king should accept her aid because she had said nothing that was contrary to the Faith and, since the country was in dire need, they "had no other hope of aid if it came not from God."[3]

Joan had two things to accomplish: lift the siege of Orléans and have the king anointed and crowned at Reims. Accompanying the army, she dressed as a man and carried a sword that the voices told her she would find behind the altar at Sainte-Catherine-de-Fierbois. On instructions from Joan, a banner was made. On one side were the words, *Jesus: Maria,* and on the other side, *In the Name of the King of Heaven.*

The French army liberated Orléans in May 1429. During the battle, Joan was wounded

A famous American missionary born in Orléans in 1607 was St. Isaac Jogues. After his ordination as a Jesuit priest in 1636, he left for North America and lived among the Huron Indians. When he was captured by the Mohawks and made a slave, he still continued on with his missionary work. He eventually escaped and came back to France in 1643, though according to Canon Law, he could not celebrate Mass because the Mohawks had mutilated his hands and sawed off his thumb. Pope Urban VIII granted him a dispensation saying, "It would be shameful that a martyr of Christ be not allowed to drink the Blood of Christ."

Isaac returned to the New World in 1644 to the very village where he had been enslaved. Isaac anticipated his death saying, "In very truth, it will be well for me, it will be happiness for me, if God will be pleased to complete the sacrifice there where He began it, if the little blood which I shed there in that land will be accepted by Him as a pledge that I would willingly shed all the blood which I bear in all the veins of my body and of my heart. In conclusion, the Iroquois people 'is the spouse of blood to me.'"[4] (This is a quote taken from Exodus 4:25, "You are a spouse of blood to me.") In 1646, Isaac was killed by a Mohawk, who later converted to Christianity and took the baptismal name of Isaac. Near this same village of Auriesville, New York, Blessed Kateri Tekawitha, the Lily of the Mohawks, was born ten years later.

Reims is the birthplace of John Baptist de la Salle, the Patron Saint of Teachers, who was born in 1651 and ordained in 1678. Rather than live a comfortable life, John gave away his fortune so he could address the educational needs of the poor. As the founder of the Institute of the Brothers of Christian Schools, John developed the revolutionary ideas of class-room teaching, instructing children in French rather than in Latin and combining secular studies with religious formation. He also estab-lished schools for the training of teachers. When he died on Good Friday, 1719, his Brothers num-bered 274 and were teaching nine thousand students.

John often encountered oppo-sition but said, "If my work does not come from God, I would con-sent to its ruin. I would join our enemies in destroying it if I thought that it did not have God for its author, or that He did not will its progress. But if He (is) its defender, let us fear nothing. He is Almighty. No arm can uproot what he has planted; no hand can snatch away what He holds in His."[5] Pope Leo XIII canonized John in 1900. His birthplace and an exhibit can be visited in Reims.

St. John Baptist de la Salle

in the breast by an arrow. A series of swift victories cleared the path to Reims. When they reached the city, the people greeted them with shouts of "Noel!" Four knights brought the holy oil (initially used by St. Remi in 496 on King Clovis) from the Ab-bey of Saint-Remi to the cathedral. On July 17, Charles was anointed the true King of France.

Joan's mission was complete but her suf-fering now began. More battles followed and Joan was wounded again. The king ignored her instructions. Joan was captured on May 23, 1430, at Compiègne by the Burgundians who sold her to the English. Her trial was conducted by Bishop Pierre Cauchon, a friend of the English. Joan was chained to her bed with soldiers in attendance at all times. She feared losing her virginity, so she stayed in the men's clothing she had worn throughout her campaigns.

The trial lasted five months. After Joan's death, a tribunal reviewed the pro-ceedings. They concluded that she was not given the opportunity to defend her-self, her statements were omitted or changed to work against her and she was confused by questions she did not understand. They also stated, "That although it was abundantly apparent to the judges that Joan had sub-mitted to the judgment and decisions of Our Holy Mother Church, and that she was so faithful a Catholic that she was allowed to receive the body of Our Lord, nevertheless, out of their excessive zeal for the En-glish, or not wishing to extricate themselves out of fear or pressure, they most unjustly condemned her as a heretic to the pains of fire. And so it was and that is the truth."[6]

St. Joan of Arc

And so she went to the stake, her hopes still unfulfilled, but never doubting for an instant that the voices were true. Five years later, the king entered Paris; twenty-two years later, England had no possessions left on French soil. She believed that He was faithful who had promised, not having received the promises, but beholding them far off and saluting them.

—Ronald Knox
Captive Flames

On the day of her execution, Joan said, "God helping me, today I shall be with Him in Paradise."[7] She placed a little homemade cross under her clothing. Friar de la Pierre brought a cross from a nearby church "to hold elevated right above her eyes up to the moment of death, so that the cross on which God hung during His life would be continually before her sight."[8] A cross in the Place du Vieux Marche in Rouen marks the spot where Joan was burned at the stake. The King of England's secretary was quoted as saying, "We are all lost because a saint has just been burned to death!" And that "even in the midst of the flames, she never stopped crying out the name of Jesus."[9]

It was reported that when the executioner collected Joan's ashes to throw them into the Seine River, he found her heart intact. Try as he might, he could not make it burn "at which he was astonished as if by a confirmed miracle."[10] Twenty-five years later, at the Rehabilitation hearings, Joan's name was cleared. She was canonized in 1920 by Pope Benedict XV and is a Patron Saint of France along with St. Thérèse of Lisieux.

St. Joan of Arc,
you were asked to do the impossible,
yet you accomplished the incredible.
You relied on prayer and the Sacraments for your strength,
and did not let human frailty deter you.
Let us emulate your courage in the decisive moments of our lives
and help us to listen to the voice of the Lord. Amen.

The Angelus

(The Angelus *bells were ringing when Joan first heard the voices. The* Angelus
is traditionally recited in the morning, at noon and in the evening)

And the Angel of the Lord declared unto Mary.
And she conceived of the Holy Spirit.
Hail Mary, full of grace…

Behold the handmaid of the Lord.
Be it done unto me according to Thy Word.
Hail Mary, full of grace…

And the Word became flesh.
And dwelt amongst us.
Hail Mary, full of grace…

Pray for us, O Holy Mother of God,
that we may be made worthy of the promises of Christ.

Pour forth, we beseech Thee O Lord, Thy grace into our hearts, that we, to
whom the Incarnation of Christ Thy Son was made known by the message of
an angel, may by His passion and cross be brought to the glory of His resurrection. We ask this through Christ Our Lord. Amen.

✣ Nine ✣
Francis de Sales

St. Francis de Sales was born into a sixteenth century world torn apart by the Protestant Reformation. Christians in Europe were no longer united under the successor of St. Peter but were divided into Catholics loyal to the Pope and Protestants who followed Martin Luther, John Calvin and others out of the Church. In the midst of this turmoil emerged a great saint who tried to unite the people under one shepherd. He is recognized today as a Doctor of the Church, the "Doctor of Love."

> *In your prayer during the day and in receiving the Blessed Sacrament, always use words of love and hope toward our Lord, such as: "You are my Father, O Lord! You are the spouse of my soul, the King of my love and the well-beloved of my soul! O good Jesus, you are my dear Master, my aid, my refuge!"*
>
> —Francis de Sales
> *Thy Will Be Done: Letters to Persons in the World*

Francis de Sales was born in 1567 in Savoy which was then independent from France. Located just south of Geneva, Switzerland, his Catholic family lived near strong Calvinist country where all signs of Catholic life had been erased. Francis was a gifted student and his father expected him to get married and have a successful career. Francis, however, had different ideas. "From my twelfth year I had resolved so firmly to belong to the Church that I would not have changed my mind for a kingdom."[1]

While in college in Paris, he had a crisis of faith. Predestination, the belief that God determines beforehand who is condemned to hell and who will live in eternal happiness, was being asserted by Calvinists and discussed by Catholics. Worried that he might be fated for eternal damnation, Francis said, "Whatever is to be Lord, at least let me love you in this life if I am unable to love you in eternity." Picking up a prayer card, he recited the *Memorarae* and all doubt and fear left him. "Have confidence, my son, I do not wish the death of the sinner, but rather he be converted and live."[2]

St. Francis de Sales

These words, taken from Ezekiel 18:23, comforted him.

After completing his studies, Francis attended the University of Padua where he studied law and, without his father's knowledge, theology. When he returned home, his elderly father tried to arrange a marriage for him. When Francis finally spoke up about his desire to become a priest, his father wept but gave his son his blessing.

Francis was immediately named Provost of the Geneva diocese, a position second in importance to the bishop. His ordination occurred in December, 1593. After celebrating his first Mass, he said, "In this first sacrifice, God took possession of my soul in an inexplicable manner."[3] He also baptized his little sister Jeanne, the last child born to his parents.

The Mass was of the utmost importance to Francis. His friend, André de Sauzea, said, "Whenever I served his Mass, I noticed that after the Consecration he stopped and was carried away with sighs in a kind of rapture and, when that lasted a while, I would point my finger to the next part of the Mass, and then he would continue." St. Jane Frances de Chantal recalled "This Divine Sacrament was his true life and his strength and, in this action, he seemed to be a man wholly transformed into God."[4]

—*Francis De Sales: Sage and Saint*

Francis' first assignment was the evangelization of the people of the Chablais, the Calvinist land just south of Lake Geneva, where only a tiny percentage of the people remained Catholic. He was helped by the example of King Henry IV of France who converted to Catholicism in 1593. Joined by his cousin Louis, Francis embarked on a four year missionary journey. It was a dangerous assignment; men were paid to kill him, he was attacked by wolves and he battled the elements on the long walks. He told Louis, "It is now that we must have courage cousin, and, provided we are not afraid, we shall see that we shall have a good yield."[5]

Francis' goal was to reestablish the celebration of the Mass as soon as possible. His efforts gradually paid off culminating in a Forty Hours devotion where, according to official records, 2300 families returned to the Faith. The Duke of Savoy said, "Here is the true apostle of the Chablais. A man whom God has sent us. . . . No one can deny that all the glory belongs to this zealous missionary."[6]

In 1602, Francis was sent to Paris where he made a lasting impression on

Jane Frances de Chantal was born in 1572 in Burgundy. After eight years of happy marriage, Jane was left a widow with four young children. When Jane met Francis for the first time, she recognized him as the man she had seen in a vision. In 1610, Jane and two other women, with the support of Francis, founded the first Visitation convent in Annecy, Savoy. When Jane died in 1641, there were eighty-seven Visitation convents. Jane was canonized in 1767 and is buried with Francis in Annecy. A biographer of Francis said, "To the ordinary person, that relationship can only be a mystery, for it went unbelievably deep in the natural as well as in the supernatural order. It was love, even human love, free and full, in which there was no taint, no suspicion, no breath of anything but their supernatural vocation. . . . One is forced back to Scripture parallels: the love of Joseph for Mary, the love of our Lord for Martha and Mary."[7]

St. Jane Frances de Chantal

the convert, King Henry IV, who described him as a "rare bird indeed; devout, learned, and a gentleman in the bargain." When he became Bishop of Geneva on December 8, 1602, his face during the ceremony was radiant. Later he said, "God deprived me of myself to make me His and to give me to my people. In other words, He changed me from what I had been for myself into what I would become for them."[8]

Francis said that everyone should receive the Eucharist as often as possible because "as the hares amidst our snowy mountains grow white from living in the snow, so by perpetually worshipping and adoring beauty, goodness, and purity in this Divine Sacrament, you, too, will become beautiful, good, and pure."

—Francis de Sales
An Introduction to the Devout Life

In 1604, Francis became the spiritual director of Jane de Chantal and, with her, founded the Visitation order, an organization for women who were unable to handle the rigors of the Carmelites and Poor Clares. A friend writing to Francis said, "It seems to me that this congregation was something that the Church needed, so that God called you in these days to raise it up. Our Lord has surely visited his people."[9]

I believe, dear Mother, if you are one mind with me, that for our coat-of-arms we will choose a heart, transfixed by two arrows and ringed by a crown of thorns. Let it be surmounted by a cross upon which will be carved the holy names of Jesus and Mary. It was our Savior, when he was dying, who gave us life by the opening of his Sacred Heart.[10]

—Francis de Sales

During his lifetime, Francis' book, *An Introduction to the Devout Life*, became a bestseller. In what was a novel idea for the time, Francis said that all people, regardless of their vocation, should try to lead a holy life. His other popular work, *Treatise on the Love of God*, was written for those who wish to grow in holiness. The key was love: love of God and a life built on the virtues of faith, hope and charity.

As bishop, Francis was deluged with paperwork. Even so, he said Mass, the Rosary, the Office, meditated for a full hour and wrote twenty or more letters every day. He died on the feast of the Holy Innocents in 1622, suffering greatly at the hands of his doctors who applied a red hot poker to his temple as a treatment. He was proclaimed a Doctor of the Church in 1877.

After his death, St. Vincent de Paul said, "Msgr. de Sales ardently wished to imitate the Son of God. So closely did he model his life on our Lord, as I myself saw, that many a time I asked myself with astonishment how a mere creature could reach so high a degree of perfection, given human frailty. . . . Recalling and meditating on his words, I felt them to be so admirable that I could only see in him the person who most nearly reproduced the Son of God living on earth."[11]

O St. Francis de Sales,
you said you were a man and a man only
yet in your human weakness you became a great saint.
I desire to grow in holiness,
yet I often think it is beyond my grasp.
Help me to realize that in my everyday life lies my key to holiness.
Dear Jesus, I pray that at the end of my life,
I will have accomplished all that you have asked of me. Amen.

A Mediation by St. Francis de Sales

Do not look forward to the changes and chances
of this life in fear;
    rather look to them with full hope that, as they arise,
God will deliver you out of them.
He has kept you hitherto;
  if you but hold fast to His dear hand,
  he will safely lead you through all things,
  and when you cannot stand,
  He will bear you in His arms.
Do not look forward to what may happen tomorrow,
  the same everlasting Father who cares for you today
  will take care of you tomorrow and everyday.
Either He will shield you from suffering,
  or He will give you strength to bear it.
Be at peace then,
  and put aside all anxious thoughts and imaginings.

✢ Ten ✢

Vincent de Paul

S t. Vincent de Paul was well-known in his day for his love for the poor. He always called them, "Our Lords, the poor." Even during the French Revolution, when mobs destroyed anything associated with the Catholic Church, a statue of Vincent in the Panthéon in Paris was saved because he was remembered as a man who cared for the poor. Long after his death, he was still a beloved figure in France.

Vincent was born into a poor farm family around 1581 in the Gascony or Landes region of southwest France. Recognized early on as a gifted child, his family sent him to the nearby town of Dax to further his education and, hopefully, the family fortunes. He studied for the priesthood in Toulouse, where he tutored children and started a school in order to pay his expenses. When he was ordained a priest in 1600, he chose to celebrate his first Mass in humble surroundings with only an acolyte and a server. Later on he said, "If I had known, when I had the rashness to present myself for ordination, as I know since, what it means to be a priest, I would far rather have spent my life tilling the soil than undertake the formidable obligations of the priestly state."[1]

St. Vincent de Paul

When in the presence of the Blessed Sacrament (Vincent) always knelt, and manifested the deepest humility. Jesus Christ was his book and his mirror in which he viewed all things. When in doubt he had recourse to his Divine model, considering what He had said or done under similar circumstances. . . . "For," he used to say, "human prudence is often deceived and wanders from the right path; but the words of eternal wisdom are infallible, and its ways straight and true."

—Bishop Bougard of Laval
History of St. Vincent de Paul

St. Vincent de Paul

The priesthood was in a sorry state in Vincent's time. The Council of Trent (1545-1563) called for the establishment of seminaries to address the issue of poorly catechized priests. Some men became priests to get ahead in the world. For awhile Vincent, too, seemed to desire a comfortable life. But, gradually, a change took place. He spent more time with the poor. He detached himself from material possessions. For awhile, he suffered from doubts against the faith but when he finally decided to devote his life in service to the poor, his crisis of faith left him for good.

While in Paris, Vincent met St. Francis de Sales who said, "He will be the holiest priest of his time." In reply, Vincent said, "I am by nature a country clod and if I had not met the Bishop of Geneva (Francis de Sales), I should have remained a bundle of thorns all of my life."[2] Vincent happily worked in a humble parish but he was persuaded to become a tutor to the children of the Count of Joigny, Philip de Gondi. Madame de Gondi placed herself under Vincent's spiritual direction.

While at the country home of the de Gondi's, Vincent was called to the bedside of a seriously ill peasant. The man later said to Madame de Gondi, "If I had not made the general confession I have just made to Monsieur Vincent, I would have been damned."[3] Realizing the need to educate the country people on the necessity of the Sacrament of Reconciliation, Vincent preached on the topic the following Sunday. The people responded and extra priests were called in to handle the resulting workload.

I have made known to you the details of (the Vincentians) daily life, but I have not revealed to you the secret of it. The secret is Jesus Christ, loved and served in the Eucharist.[4]

—Father Etienne

Feeling that he was called to serve "poor, country folk," Vincent secretly left the de Gondi's and moved to a poor parish in Châtillon-les-Dombes. While he was vesting for Mass one day, "word was brought to me that in an isolated house . . . everyone was ill . . . and that all were in indescribable need. I had only to mention this in the sermon when God touched the hearts of those who heard me and they found themselves deeply moved with

Louise de Marillac (1591-1660) had suffered much in her life before she met Vincent. She was born out of wedlock to an unidentified woman but her father was the well-known Louis de Marillac who called Louise "his greatest consolation." She was placed in the care of an aunt in the Abbey of Poissy where she received her education. Of her early life, she said, "God who has granted me so many graces, led me to understand that it was his holy will that I go to Him by way of the cross. His goodness chose to mark me with it from my birth and he has hardly ever left me, at any age, without some occasion of suffering."

In 1613, Louise married Antoine Le Gras, the secretary to Queen Marie de Medici and later that year they had a son, Michael. When her husband died after a long illness in 1625, Louise, who had taken a vow of widowhood, became involved with the works of Vincent de Paul. In 1633, they co-founded the Sisters or Daughters of Charity.

Louise said, "If you completely entrust everything to the guidance of divine providence and love the most holy will of God, this will contribute greatly to your peace of mind and heart. In fact, this is one of the most essential practices I know of for growth in holiness."[5] Two well-known Daughters of Charity are Sts. Catherine Labouré and Elizabeth Ann Seton, the first American-born saint.

St. Louise de Marillac

compassion for these poor, afflicted ones."[6] So generous were his parishioners that Vincent realized that many needy families could be helped with a little organization, so he formed a confraternity called the Ladies of Charity.

Madame de Gondi, realizing the good work that Vincent had accomplished on their estate, granted him a large endowment to use for missionary work across the countryside. This was the beginning of the Congregation of the Mission or Vincentians. With Louise de Marillac, he also formed a community of women totally devoted to the poor. They were not cloistered in prayer, but remained out in the world, a unique concept for the times. Louise said, "It is of little use for us to run about the streets with bowls of soup if we do not make the love of God the object of our effort. If we let go of the thought that the poor are His members, our love for them will soon grow cold."[7]

These first Daughters of Charity, the "gray nuns," worked in hospitals, fed victims of war, housed orphans and ministered to prisoners. They also cared for abandoned children who were shunned by society as tainted by their parents' sins. These children, Vincent said, "suffer for something of which they are innocent. If you protect and maintain them you may hope for wonderful blessings. You blot out your past and present sins and in some ways those of the future. . . . You put yourself in the happy position of being able to hold up your head on Judgment Day."[8]

Holy Communion with the Body of Jesus Christ causes us truly to participate in the joy of the Communion of Saints in Paradise. . . . Just as God sees Himself united to man in the heaven of hypostatic union of the Word made Flesh, so he wanted such a union on earth so that the human race would never again be separated from him.[9]

—St. Louise de Marillac

Vincent preferred to be with the poor but he was greatly esteemed by the Royal Family. King Louis XIII summoned Vincent to his deathbed. He was a counselor to Queen Anne of Austria. Louis XIV wrote a letter supporting Vincent's canonization. However, he was still a man of the people, at one point distributing soup to over 15,000 war refugees a day. He also ransomed 1200 slaves from North Africa and sent missionaries to Poland, Madagascar and Ireland, where the first Vincentian was martyred.

Vincent de Paul and Louise de Marillac both died in 1660. His incorrupt body rests at the motherhouse of the Congregation of the Mission at 95 rue de Sévres in Paris. His heart is in a reliquary at the Motherhouse of the Daughters of Charity, 140 rue du Bac. In this chapel in 1830, Catherine Labouré had visions of the heart of St. Vincent. In 1833, Bl. Frederic Ozanam founded the St. Vincent de Paul Society which carries on his work today. In 1885, Pope Leo XIII named Vincent the Patron Saint of Charitable Workers while in 1960, Louise was named Patron Saint of Christian Social Workers.

O Vincent de Paul,
servant of the poor
Help me to see that my talents, possessions and life
are gifts from God to be used in His service.
Inspired by your example,
let me entrust all that I have to Him,
recognizing that to those who have been given much,
much will be asked. Amen.

The Nicene Creed

(St. Vincent de Paul placed these words over his heart and touched them when he suffered from temptations against the faith. The words were mainly drawn up by the Council of Nicaea in 325 and added to by the Council of Constantinople in 381)

We believe in one God,
  the Father, the Almighty,
    maker of heaven and earth,
    and all that is seen and unseen.
We believe in one Lord, Jesus Christ,
    the only Son of God.
    Eternally begotten of the Father,
    God from God, Light from Light,
    true God from true God,
    begotten not made, one in being with the Father.
    Through him all things were made.
For us men and for our salvation
    he came down from heaven:
by the power of the Holy Spirit
    he was born of the Virgin Mary,
        and became man.
For our sake he was crucified under Pontius Pilate;
    he suffered, died, and was buried.
    On the third day he rose again
        in fulfillment of the Scriptures;
    he ascended into heaven
        and is seated at the right hand of the Father.
He will come again in glory to judge the living and the dead,
    and his kingdom will have no end.
We believe in the Holy Spirit, the Lord, the giver of life,
    who proceeds from the Father and the Son.
    With the Father and the Son he is worshipped and glorified.
    He has spoken through the Prophets.
    We believe in one holy catholic and apostolic Church.
    We acknowledge one baptism for the forgiveness of sins.
    We look for the resurrection of the dead,
        and the life of the world to come. Amen.

✤ *Eleven* ✤

John Francis Regis

John Francis Regis was one of the great missionaries of France. He lived a short life, ordained just years before his death, but his burial site became a popular pilgrimage site. St. John Vianney, on his deathbed, sent an emissary to the grave of John Francis to give thanks for all he had accomplished as a priest. St. Rose Philippine Duchesne prayed to know the will of God at the shrine of St. Regis and became a famous American missionary. Mathias Loras vowed to become a missionary if his sister was cured after praying at the shrine and later became the first bishop of Dubuque, Iowa. In life and in death, John Francis' influence produced dramatic results.

John Francis was born in 1597 in Fontcouverte in Languedoc to a noble family. He was sent to the Jesuit school at Béziers and, in 1616, entered the Jesuit novitiate at Toulouse. A teacher for six years, he was very popular with his students who secretly revered him. One of his students said, "There was no way of not paying full attention to the words that flowed from his lips. Each of us, in incredible silence, hung on the least words he spoke with so much ardor, especially when this thought was to inspire us with devotion to the Mother of God and with love of the most Holy Eucharist."[1]

After his ordination, John Francis assisted plague victims in Toulouse and

St. John Francis Regis

eventually moved on to Montpellier to begin his missionary work. During the Religious Wars (1562-1598) between Catholics and Protestants, the area had been under the control of the Calvinists (Huguenots) and many churches were destroyed and priests and lay people murdered. The few Catholics who remained in the area were poorly catechized and indifferent to their faith.

Like the Curé of Ars (St. John Vianney), who in fact two centuries later modeled much of his apostolate on that of his patron Regis, the young missionary inaugurated his apostolic endeavors by means of simple, un-adorned, matter-of-fact talks in church. The same sincerity and unmistakable appeal which was later destined to make little Ars the focal point of hundreds of pilgrimages, appeared with startling freshness in the sermons of Regis. One had only to listen to the frank, direct, living messages that arose from the heart of this man of God, in order to be convinced that here was the word of God and the road to life.

—Albert S. Foley, SJ
St. Regis: Social Crusader

The success John Francis realized in Montpellier was typical of what he would accomplish during his subsequent missionary journeys. He preached, befriended the rich and the poor, and prevailed upon the wealthy to provide for the needy. He provided the poor with free medical services and intervened in court for them. He established safe places, later called refuges, for prostitutes who wished to reform their lives. He heard thousands of confessions and established Confraternities of the Blessed Sacrament. He was humble, courageous and virtuous, and willingly suffered on behalf of his flock.

Le-Puy became the base for John Francis' last activities from 1634-1640. He achieved success but not without a cost. He was subject to physical assaults, taunting and smear campaigns. A bishop, believing the false stories, dismissed him from his diocese though he was quickly recalled after the truth became known. John Francis simply said, "I do not doubt that my many faults have escaped my notice."[2]

The area around Toulouse is associated with one of the Church's greatest figures, St. Dominic Guzman (d. 1221). Dominic, the great Spanish saint who founded the Order of Preachers or Dominicans, accompanied a bishop to southern France to combat the Albigensian heresy. According to tradition, Our Lady told him at the sanctuary of Notre Dame de la Dreche near Albi, "Preach my Psalter and you will obtain an abundant harvest."[3] The Psalter was a collection of the 150 psalms. Saying a Hail Mary for each of the 150 psalms and adding meditations on the life, death and resurrection of Jesus developed it into the rosary devotion we know today. There is no solid evidence attributing the rosary (from the Latin *rosarium* meaning bed of roses) to Dominic, but several popes including Leo XIII and Pius V have recognized the Dominicans as having a special historical and custodial role in the spreading of the devotion.

St. Thomas Aquinas, a spiritual son of Dominic, is also associated with Toulouse. Thomas taught for many years at the University of Paris during the reign of St. Louis and, though he died in Italy at the Cistercian Monaster of Fossanova in 1274, his relics reside today in the Jacobin Church in Toulouse where St. John Francis Regis was a frequent visitor.

John Francis' work with prostitutes caused him the most trouble. He established a refuge for them at Le-Puy as a place where they could safely live together in a community. One man told John Francis that he would kill him

Le-Puy-en-Velay is famous for its ancient shrine to the Blessed Virgin Mary, one of the oldest in Christendom. The city was also one of the four main starting points for travelers on the road to the shrine of St. James at Santiago de Compostela in Spain (the others being Vézelay, Arles and Paris/Chartres). Today, a fifty-five foot statue of Our Lady towers over the valley on one of the volcanic peaks and a replica (the original was burned during the French Revolution) of the ancient statue of the Black Virgin can be seen in the cathedral.

The beautiful Rocamadour, another ancient pilgrimage site located north of Toulouse, was also a stop on the road to Santiago de Compostela. One legend says that Zacchaeus, the tax collector named in Luke 19:2, lived here in a hermitage that he named "Amadour" (the man who loves God). Traditionally, pilgrims used to climb the 216 steps of the Great Staircase on their knees to reach their ultimate destination, the Notre-Dame chapel, containing the twelfth century statue of Our Lady of Rocamadour, the Black Virgin.

Rocamadour

if his girl was not returned to him. John Francis asked for time to say an Act of Contrition and then said, "Now strike me. But that girl is free and belongs to Christ." The man lost his nerve and fled. Once a man lured John Francis to a church with the intention of stabbing him. John Francis said, "I know your conscience is steeped in crimes, but God's mercy far outreaches their number and heinousness. God waits to pardon you. Here, enter the confessional. Conceal nothing. It will be easy, and I promise you peace of soul."[4] The man went to Confession and brought in his associates who also experienced a spiritual conversion under the care of John Francis.

John Francis wanted to be a missionary in Canada but was told, "Canada for you will be the Vivarais," so he continued to trek through the remote areas of southern France to reach his lost sheep. Usually he "would go straight to the church to pay his respects to his Sacramental Lord,"[5] sometimes kneeling in the snow if the door was locked. His visits were often commemorated later with a chapel or a cross of St. Regis. Trying to explain his success with the people, John Francis said, "God is surely great, and I am at a loss to explain how it all came about."[6]

To care for the poor, John Francis kept a supply of wheat on hand to give to the hungry. One day, the woman in charge told him that the wheat had run out. John Francis told her to look again. To her astonishment, the bin was full. John Francis told her that the granaries of God are never empty. Two hundred years later, St. John Vianney was in a similar situation. "I had a great number of orphans to feed and in the storehouse was only a handful of wheat. It occurred to me that St. Francis Regis, who had fed the poor miraculously, might well do it again. I had a relic of the saint and placed it among the wheat which remained. And I had the children pray. And the storehouse room was full."[7]

During the last months of his life, John Francis continued on his strenuous journeys, hearing nine thousand confessions in under four months and preaching three to four times a day. He had a premonition of his death and said that he would die at Christmas time in La Louvesc. He died during a mission there on December 31, 1640, at age forty-three. He was canonized by Pope Clement XII in 1737, on the same day as St. Vincent de Paul.

A good summation of his life is contained in a statement written by the General Council of Le-Puy after his death: "Our churches, our prisons, our hospitals would speak if we did not. Our churches would say that he was a man of God through and through; our hospitals that he was a man of the poor; and our prisons that he carried mercy into the house of justice. . . . One only had to be wretched to see Father Regis at his side; he poured himself out for the poor, and if he had possessed as much finances and supplies as charity, he would have made works of mercy come to an end for lack of miseries among the poor."[8]

In the persons of these imploring mendicants, Francis discerned the vision beautiful, not in legend but in reality. He served them wholeheartedly . . . in the realization that Christ was being tended in them. This is one of the reasons why men noted that Francis seemed entranced in his work for them, enrapt in it as though it were a most absorbing contemplation, an all but sacramental handling of Christ's own body.

—Albert S. Foley, s.j.
St. Regis: Social Crusader

The shrine of John Francis Regis at La Louvesc attracted many pilgrims and the church was designated as a basilica. It was at La Louvesc that St. Thérèse Couderc founded the Congregation of Our Lady of the Retreat of the Cenacle. Cenacle Centers have spread throughout the world as places of retreat and prayer. St. Thérèse was canonized a saint in 1970.

O Lord,
let us always remember that our actions and thoughts
can have an impact far beyond our imaginings.
As St. John Francis Regis continued to inspire others
many years after his death,
may our lives, too, be a true reflection
of Christ in the world. Amen.

Act of Oblation by St. Thérèse Couderc [9]

(St. Thérèse Couderc founded the Congregation of Our Lady
of the Retreat of the Cenacle)

Lord Jesus, I unite myself to your perpetual, unceasing, universal sacrifice. I offer myself to you every day of my life and every moment of every day, according to your most holy and adorable will.

You have been the victim of my salvation,
I wish to be the victim of your love.

Accept my desire, take my offering, graciously hear my prayer:
let me live by love, let me die of love,
and let my last heartbeat be an act of the most perfect love. Amen.

✤ Twelve ✤

Margaret Mary Alacoque

S t. Margaret Mary Alacoque is intimately associated with the Sacred Heart of Jesus because it was to her that our Lord entrusted the mission of spreading the devotion to His Sacred Heart. Margaret Mary prepared for this task by living a life of obedience, first to her family, then to her superiors in the convent. Her days were often filled with misery and humiliation but she said, "I only find true happiness in crosses, contempt and suffering."[1]

My Divine Savior has given me to understand that those who labor for the salvation of souls will have the gift of touching even the most hardened hearts and will have wonderful success in their work if they themselves are filled with tender devotion to His divine heart.[2]

—St. Margaret Mary Alacoque

Born in 1647 on the feast of St. Mary Magdalene at L'Hautecour in Burgundy, Margaret Mary made a vow of perpetual chastity to the Lord when she was very young. In 1655, her father died and, eventually, Margaret Mary was sent to a school run by the Poor Clares. Beginning in 1657, she was bedridden for several years with an illness that only lifted when she made another vow that, if the Blessed Mother cured her, she would one day become one of

her daughters. Margaret Mary and her mother still lived in the family home but her relatives treated them as lowly servants. She spent many nights weeping before a crucifix and found all of her "pleasure and consolation in the Most Blessed Sacrament of the altar."[3]

As Margaret Mary grew older, her family tried to arrange a suitable marriage for her but she had not forgotten her vow to become a nun. "Dearest mother's tears were proving too much for me," she wrote, "I was beginning to weaken." One day after receiving Communion, the Lord confirmed her

St. Margaret Mary   vocation and she felt "peace of soul at last."[4] In the face of her determination, her family consented to her vocation. She did not have a particular order in mind but, when she arrived at the Visitation convent in Paray-le-Monial, she heard these words in her heart, "This is where I want you."[5] The emblem of the Visitation order, adopted by St. Francis de Sales, was a heart pierced by two arrows, surrounded by the Crown of Thorns. Francis once said, "Truly our little congregation is the work of the heart of Jesus."[6]

What I looked forward to most about going into a convent was being able to go often to Communion. At home, they would only let me go on rare occasions. Frequent Communion—that was the height of happiness for me! If only they would have let me spend whole nights alone with the Blessed Sacrament! Though I was a very timid girl, I felt quite safe there; my mind was so full of the happiness it gave me, I could not think of anything else.

—St. Margaret Mary
The Autobiography of St. Margaret Mary

On December 27, 1673, Margaret Mary received the first of the great revelations from the Lord in which He called her the "beloved disciple of His Sacred Heart."[7] She was praying in front of the Blessed Sacrament when "I forgot all about myself, and where I was, it was so intense; I simply gave myself up to the Spirit of God."[8] Jesus told her that His Heart, so full of love, was unable to contain the flames of this burning love any longer. She was chosen to reveal this Heart to the world, a Heart containing all of the graces needed for salvation.

The second revelation occurred in 1674, though the exact date is uncertain, as Margaret Mary again prayed before the Blessed Sacrament. "He was a blaze of glory—his five wounds shining like five suns, flames issuing from all parts of his human form, especially from his divine breast" which He opened to reveal the source of those flames, "His utterly affectionate and lovable heart."[9] But this love was received by the world with ingratitude and indifference. Jesus asked Margaret Mary to atone for this neglect by receiving the Eucharist as often as possible, in particular on the First Friday of every month. He also asked that she pray with Him for one hour every Thursday night, sharing in His agony as in the garden of Gethsemane.

No fervent soul has ever relaxed (in their spirituality) who did not first (stop) receiving the Holy Eucharist. If I found that when going frequently to Communion I became no better, was still just as weak, just as prone to evil, just as indifferent about sin, I should conclude, not that I ought to leave off going, but that I ought to receive Our Lord with better dispositions. I should see if my confessions were wanting in sincerity, contrition or purpose of amendment.[10]

—St. Claude de la Colombière

The man destined to make Margaret Mary's revelations known to the world, Claude de la Colombière, was born in 1641 in St. Symphorien d'Ozon south of Lyons. No record exists of his baptism for the Curé noted that the dog had eaten the pages! He was ordained a Jesuit priest and a few year later became superior of the Jesuit house in Paray-le-Monial. Mother de Saumise, the Superior of the Visitation convent, asked him to interview Margaret Mary about her revelations which some considered to be hallucinations. When Margaret Mary first saw Claude, an inner voice told her, "This is he whom I have sent you." [11] She rebuffed him once but, during their second meeting, she opened her heart to him. Claude believed that her revelations were truly from God and on June 21, 1675, he consecrated himself to the Sacred Heart of Jesus.

Claude devoted the rest of his life to directing souls and propagating the devotion to the Sacred Heart, even in Protestant England where he was assigned as the chaplain to the Catholic Duchess of York. He was imprisoned for promoting Catholicism and banished from the country. His health was broken as a result of his treatment and he died in 1682. Claude's life was best summed up by Margaret Mary who wrote, "Father de la Colombière's talent is to lead souls to God." [12]

St. Claude de la Colombiére

During the last revelation, Jesus asked that the Friday after the octave of Corpus Christi be "set apart as a special feast in honor of my Heart—a day on which to receive me in Holy Communion and make a solemn act of reparation for the indignities I have received in the Blessed Sacrament while exposed on the altars of the world. I promise you, too, that I shall open my heart to all who honor me in this way." [13]

Jansenism, a heretical movement that taught that the Eucharist was reserved for only the most worthy, was prevalent at the time in France. Margaret Mary's mission "was to proclaim the condescending love of God by showing the world his Sacred Heart. The God who was made Man in Jesus was not a fear-inspiring despot whom no one dared approach, but a God of love, who, showing to man His human Heart . . . invited them to come to Him lovingly, without fear, like children to their Father." [14] Pope Leo XIII said that nothing can be more important than to see devotion to the Sacred Heart of Jesus and the Holy Eucharist grow everyday.

For ten years after these revelations, no action was taken to promote this devotion and Margaret Mary endured great suffering and humiliations from those who did not believe in her revelations. This changed when Claude de la Colombière's writings, in which he declared the revelations to be genuine, were published after his death. Paray-le-Monial celebrated the first feast of the Sacred Heart and Pope Clement XIII authorized the liturgical observance of the feast in 1765. Pope Pius IX extended the feast to the entire Church in 1856 and in 1899, Pope Leo XIII consecrated the human race to the Sacred Heart of Jesus.

The revelations made to St. Margaret Mary added nothing new into Catholic doctrine. The significance of these revelations lies in this, that Christ the Lord— showing His Sacred Heart—willed in an extraordinary and special way to call the minds of men to the contemplation and veneration of the mystery of God's most merciful love for the human race. And so in this special manifestation, in repeated and clear words, Christ pointed to His Heart as the symbol by which men are drawn to recognize and acknowledge His love, and at the same time constituted it as the sign and pledge of His mercy and His grace for the needs of the Church in our time.

—Pope Pius XII
Haurietas Aquas

Margaret Mary died in 1690 and was canonized by Pope Benedict XV in 1920. Her relics are in the Chapel of the Visitation in Paray-le-Monial. The tomb of Claude de la Colombière, who was canonized by Pope John Paul II, is in the Jesuit chapel. The town's Romanesque Basilica of the Sacred Heart (c. 1100) is a replica, on a smaller scale, of the Benedictine Abbey at Cluny. Nearby is also the ecumenical community of Taizé, founded by Brother Roger in 1940, and well-known throughout the world for its meditative music.

O Margaret Mary,
help me to imitate your life of humble obedience.
You did not seek to do your will on earth;
rather you conformed your life to the Cross.
Help me to willingly offer reparation
for my sins and the sins of the world.
May I place all my trust
in the Sacred Heart of Jesus. Amen.

Consecration to the Sacred Heart

(Composed by St. Margaret Mary)

I give and consecrate myself
to the Sacred Heart of Our Lord Jesus Christ.
I offer my body and my life,
my actions, works and sufferings,
and it is my desire therefore
to use no part of my being
save in honoring, loving and glorifying Him.
It is my steadfast purpose to belong only to Him,
to do everything for love of Him,
and to renounce absolutely all that could displease Him.

Therefore, I take You, O Sacred Heart,
as the sole object of my love, as the protector of my life,
as the safeguard of my salvation,
and the remedy of my frailty and fickleness,
for You can make good all that I have done wrongly,
and You will be my sure refuge at the hour of death.
Be, O loving Heart, my justification before God the Father,
and turn aside from me His wrath,
which I have so justly deserved.

I put all my confidence in You,
for I fear my own wickedness and weakness,
and hope all from Your goodness.
Destroy in me all that might displease or oppose You.
Let Your pure love be so firmly impressed upon my heart
that I may never forget You, and never be separated from You.

I ask You for Your mercy,
allow my name to be inscribed on Your heart,
for I wish all my happiness and my glory to consist in living
and dying as Your slave. Amen.

✤ Thirteen ✤
Louis de Montfort

Louis de Montfort is best known today for his writings on the Blessed Virgin Mary. In his lifetime, however, he was known as a great missionary. The Vendée, the area in the west of France where he conducted his missions, defended the Catholic Church at great cost during the French Revolution. Pope John Paul II linked Louis and the Vendéans when he spoke at the tomb of Louis in 1996: "You who were born in this land of the Vendée . . . are the heirs of the men and women who were courageous enough to remain faithful to the Church of Jesus Christ at a time when its freedom and independence were threatened."[1]

Louis was born in Montfort-La-Cane in Brittany in 1673. The oldest child of eight, he had a devotion to Mary and took her name at Confirmation. "Louis Marie," said his uncle, had "such a horror of vice and such an inclination to virtue that you would have thought him immune to Adam's sin. . . . The words 'God alone' were written on his heart."[2] Louis was an excellent student and at age twelve he was sent to a Jesuit school in Rennes. He believed he had a calling to the priesthood and eventually left for St. Sulpice Seminary in Paris.

St. Louis de Montfort

Louis was a big man who was misunderstood and underestimated by those around him. His superiors were leery of his piety and his self-imposed penances. He kept apart, not out of aloofness but because he could walk only one road, the one he believed led to Jesus Christ. The influence of Jansenism kept many away from the Sacraments, but Louis embraced his faith ardently. His time in the seminary was difficult but he looked upon his "little crosses" as his road to perfection. For the rest of his life, he embraced the Cross and saw, in the suffering of others, the living image of the crucified Christ.

Louis consecrated himself to Mary while in the seminary, as the sure path to Jesus. "Mary presents our good works to Jesus," he wrote. "She does not keep anything we offer for herself, as if she were the last end, but unfailingly gives everything to Jesus. . . . When anyone praises and blesses her, she sings today as she did on the day Elizabeth praised her, 'My soul glorifies the Lord.'"[3]

True devotion to Mary is an easy, short, perfect and safe road to perfection, which means union with Christ. To a Christian, perfection is nothing else than such a union. It is an easy road. It was opened by Jesus when he came to us. The road of Mary is gentle, peaceful. One finds there, it is true, great difficulties and fierce battles. But our mother is ever near, to light the darkness, to clear away doubts, to give strength, to banish fear, to help in every way. . . . The road is the most perfect one by which to reach Christ and be united to Him.[4]

—St. Louis de Montfort

On the day of his ordination in 1700, Louis spent most of his time praying before the Blessed Sacrament. His dream was to become a missionary but he was assigned to a hospital in Poitiers which in those days was a home for paupers, orphans, prostitutes, criminals and the mentally ill. He gathered a few receptive women into a prayer group forming the beginning of the Daughters of Wisdom, an order he co-founded with Blessed Marie Louise Trichet. Louis wrote, "To know Jesus Christ, incarnate Wisdom, is to know all we need. To presume to know everything and not know Him is to know nothing at all."[5] Louis' attempts to reform the hospital were welcomed by some but

In 1789, after the French royal family was imprisoned by the revolutionary forces, all Church property was confiscated by the state. The following year, the Civil Constitution of the Clergy became law. This law made the Church beholden to the state in matters of diocesan organization and selection of bishops and pastors. All clergymen were required to uphold this law. Only a few took the oath. As a result, the Catholic Church was targeted for persecution and many priests and religious were murdered.

One area of France did not stand by as this bloodshed unfolded. South of Nantes, in the area called the Vendée, the people rose up and fought the National Guard who came to conscript them into the army. Inspired by St. Louis de Montfort, who had evangelized the region seventy years before, the Vendéans won stunning victories against superior forces. Even though they were ultimately defeated with the loss of an estimated 300,000 lives, their dying was not in vain. A concordat signed in 1801 between Napoleon, who admired the Vendéans, and Pope Pius VII became known as the Victory of the Vendée. When Pope John Paul II visited the area in 1996, he said, "The people of the Vendée remained attached to their parishes and their priests despite the cruelty of the persecution. They had a real hunger for the Eucharist; at the risk of their lives, they desired to take part in Mass and to receive the Bread of Life."[6]

Blessed Marie Louise Trichet was born in 1684 in Poitiers and first encountered Louis in the confessional. Marie Louise said that her sister had sent her to him, but Louis said, "No, you are mistaken: it was the Blessed Virgin." Marie Louise worked at a hospital in Poitiers for ten years until Louis asked her to join him at La Rochelle to begin the work of the Daughters of Wisdom. A school for the poor was founded and the first vocations came. In 1716, while the order was still in its infancy, Louis died. It was left to Marie Louise to bring to fruition what Louis had put down on paper. By the time she died, the quiet but determined Marie Louise had established thirty-six communities.

A biographer, Benedetta Papasogli, describes Marie Louise at the end of her life as a "living tabernacle" for the Lord. She died in 1759 on the same day and in the same place as Louis de Montfort. After her death, Father Besnard wrote that she was "a living copy of the virtues of Jesus Christ, Eternal Wisdom."[7] Louis Marie and Marie Louise are buried side by side in the church at St. Laurent-sur-Sévre. She was beatified by Pope John Paul II in 1993.

resented by those who took advantage of the poor and defenseless. After a stormy tenure, he left Poitiers and found work in Salpêtriére Hospital in Paris. Meanwhile, his friends from Poitiers wrote to his old spiritual director with the plea, "By the death and passion of Jesus, for the glory and the love of God, please send back our beloved chaplain, our angel, Father de Montfort, the shepherd who so dearly loved his sheep."[8]

Eternal Wisdom, on the other hand, wished to prove his love for man by dying in his place in order to save him, but on the other hand, he could not bear the thought of leaving him. So he devised a marvelous way of dying and living at the same time, and of abiding with man until the end of time. So, in order to fully satisfy his love, he instituted the sacrament of the Holy Eucharist and went to the extent of changing and overturning nature itself. He does not conceal himself under a sparkling diamond or some other precious stone, because he does not want to abide with man in an ostentatious manner. But he hides himself under the appearance of a small piece of bread—man's ordinary nourishment—so that when received he might enter the heart of man and there take his delight."

—St. Louis de Montfort
Love of Eternal Wisdom in *God Alone*

Louis was welcomed back to Poitiers but it was a short stay. His zeal still created enemies. He asked Marie Louise Trichet to stay at the hospital; a stay which lasted ten years until she and Catherine Brunet, the second Daughter of Wisdom, joined him in La Rochelle. Louis meanwhile received permission from the bishop to be a roving missionary where "he introduced the rosary, held processions and parades, preached to tremendous crowds, founded lay apostolates of various kinds—and here and there repaired a ruined church or chapel." He was well-known for his gentleness in the confessional and once stated, "If I am too lenient with sinners, I will gladly suffer for it in purgatory. I would rather suffer thus than be harsh with them, or sparing of God's infinite mercy."[9]

In 1706, Louis went to Rome where St. Giuseppe Maria Tomasi arranged for a meeting between Louis and Pope Clement XI. The Holy Father told him that his vocation was to be a "Missionary Apostolic" to the people of France. He would spend the rest of his life walking the roads of western France, begging for food and often using a rock for a pillow and twigs for a mattress. He eventually became a Third Order Dominican, following in the footsteps of another great preacher, St. Dominic.

The Holy Sacrifice of the Mass gives boundless honor to the Most Blessed Trinity because it represents the passion of Jesus Christ and because through the Mass we offer God the merits of Our Lord's obedience, of His sufferings and of His Precious Blood. The whole of the heavenly court also receives an accidental joy from the Mass. Several doctors of the Church—together with St. Thomas Aquinas— tell us that, for the same reason, all the blessed in Heaven rejoice in the communion of the faithful because the Blessed Sacrament is a memorial of the passion and death of Jesus Christ, and that by means of it men share in its fruits and work out their salvation.

—St. Louis de Montfort
The Secret of the Rosary

St. Louis de Montfort

Louis encountered much hostility but he was never one to flinch from proclaiming the Gospel. The Vendée was not known for the religious fervor of the people. Louis encountered throngs of people in the "public squares and the streets and the taverns, doing their best to drown the voice of the preacher in their blasphemous and profane songs. In some places a whole population will greet him with groans and hisses, and take up stones to stone him; in others he will be led off to prison, or smitten in the face, or beaten, or threatened with the dagger or the sword, and even this in the sanctuary of God. Yet . . . he will leave behind him a people rooted in Christ."[10]

Louis died at St. Laurent-sur-Sévre in 1716 with a crucifix in one hand and a statue of Mary in the other. He was canonized by Pope Pius XII in 1947. He is most famous today for two books he wrote on Mary; *True Devotion to the Blessed Virgin* and *The Secret of Mary*. These manuscripts lay undiscovered in a chest for over a hundred years until a priest came across them in 1842. Pope John Paul II's motto, *Totus Tuus* (Totally Yours), was inspired by Louis. Today, many people consecrate themselves to the Blessed Virgin using a prayer composed by Louis.

> *O Louis de Montfort,*
> *you know what it is like to be misunderstood and wronged,*
> *yet you always accepted these setbacks as "little crosses" to be loved.*
> *Help me to see God's hand in all my difficulties.*
> *Jesus, help me to love my "little crosses."*
> *Mary, lead me to Jesus. Amen.*

Act of Consecration to Jesus Christ, the Incarnate Wisdom, by the Hands of Mary
(Excerpt, composed by St. Louis de Montfort)

I (N. N.) an unfaithful sinner, renew and ratify through you my baptismal promises. I renounce forever Satan, his empty promises, and his evil designs, and I give myself completely to Jesus Christ, the incarnate Wisdom, to carry my cross after Him for the rest of my life, and to be more faithful to Him than I have been until now.

This day, with the whole court of heaven as witness, I choose you, Mary, as my Mother and Queen. I surrender and consecrate myself to you, body and soul, as your slave, with all that I possess, both spiritual and material, even including the value of all my good actions, past, present and to come. I give you the full right to dispose of me and all that belongs to me, without reservations, in whatever way you please, for the greater glory of God in time and throughout eternity.

O admirable Mother, present me to your dear Son as his slave now and for always, so that he who redeemed me through you, will now receive me through you. Mother of mercy, grant me the favor of obtaining the true Wisdom of God, and so make me one of those whom you love, teach and guide, whom you nourish and protect as your children and slaves.

Virgin most faithful, make me in everything so committed a disciple, imitator, and slave of Jesus, your Son, incarnate Wisdom, that I may become, through your intercession and example, fully mature with the fullness of his glory. Amen.

❧ *Fourteen* ❧
The Martyrs of Compiègne

Compiègne, located just north of Paris on the river Oise, is a site rich in history. It was here that Joan of Arc was captured, the Germans surrendered to the French in 1918 and, in 1794, sixteen Carmelite nuns were arrested during the French Revolution and taken to their deaths in Paris. Inspired by a prophecy written years earlier by a Carmelite nun, these sisters offered themselves as a holocaust—a total offering to the Lord—to end the bloodshed of the French Revolution.

When the French Revolution broke out in 1789 with the falling of the Bastille prison, the special relationship that had existed between the Church and the "most Christian" kings of France was destroyed. This relationship began with the baptism and anointing of Clovis as king by St. Remi in 496 in Reims. Joan of Arc recognized Charles VII as king only after he was anointed with the same oil used on Clovis. When the revolutionaries smashed the vial containing the holy oil, it symbolized a break with their Christian past.

The first Carmelite convent in France was founded in 1604 through the efforts of Madame Acarie, who became a lay Carmelite after her husband's death. The Carmel at Compiègne was founded in 1641, the fifty-third Carmel in France. The Carmelites had close ties to the royal family. Louis XV's daughter became a Carmelite and Queen Marie Antoinette paid the dowry of Madame Lidoine, the future prioress of the Carmelite martyrs. Madame Lidoine's religious name was Teresa, after St. Teresa of Avila, their foundress.

Sometime after Madame Lidoine was elected prioress in 1786, she came across a century old manuscript that described a vision in which the community was asked to follow the Lamb. Madame Lidoine associated this vision with the Passover Lamb whose blood was poured out to save the Israelites, and with Jesus, the Lamb of God, whose blood was shed to save all people from sin and death. "For our paschal lamb, Christ, has been sacrificed" (1 Cor 5:7). She believed that this vision pertained to their community.

After the Revolution broke out, the new government focused their attention on the Church. Convents were closed, nuns were forced to wear civilian clothes, religious vows were forbidden and Church property was confiscated.

St. Julie Billiart

The revolutionaries came up with a ten day work week to eliminate Sundays. During a two-day period in 1792, 250 priests who refused to take an oath of allegiance to the state were killed. One estimate is that 30,000 priests sought safety in other countries. In September of the same year, the Carmelites of Compiégne were ousted from their monastery.

Madame Lidoine presented the idea to the sisters of offering themselves as a holocaust to end the bloodshed of the Revolution. "Having meditated much on this subject, I have thought of making an act of consecration by which the community would offer itself as a sacrifice to appease the anger of God, so that the divine peace of His dear Son would be brought into the world, returned to the Church and State."[1] The sisters agreed and began to recite a daily act of consecration.

Somewhere between six months and two years before their death, (the Martyrs of Compiègne) recited a daily prayer in which they offered themselves as martyrs in order to save the lives of their countrymen. These were not melodramatic women fulfilling a dream of heroism. This was a Christian community who prayerfully and painstakingly discerned and verified a vocation to martyrdom.

—Fr. Richard Veras
Magnificat, July 2002

Another saint who took refuge in Compiègne was St. Julie Billiart who was born in 1751 in Cuvilly in Picardy. She was an intelligent girl who was allowed to receive her first Holy Communion before other children her age. Julie helped her family by doing needlework and sewing, sometimes for the Carmelites at Compiègne. In 1774, a shot was fired through the window of her father's shop which did not hit her but still frightened her to the point of paralysis. Later, she often lost the ability to speak. Despite her disability, she received Communion daily and instructed children and adults in the Faith.

During the Revolution, she found hiding places for priests who refused to swear allegiance to the state and became wanted herself. She fled to Compiègne hidden in a straw wagon and it was there that she had a dream in which she saw her future spiritual daughters with Jesus. When a young woman later joined the congregation, Julie used to say, "I saw you at Compiègne!"[2] In 1794, she moved to Amiens where a group of women gathered around her, including Françoise Blin de Bourdon. This was the beginning of the congregation called the Sisters of Notre Dame de Namur. It was during this period that Julie prayed a novena and was cured of her paralysis on the feast of the Sacred Heart. Julie died in Namur, Belgium in 1816. Her favorite expression was, "How good is the good God!"

On June 22, 1794, the Carmelites were arrested and later taken to Paris. On July 16, the feast of Our Lady of Mount Carmel, they were accused of conspiracy against the Republic, in possession of hearts (the symbol of the resistance fighters who chose the Sacred Heart of Jesus as their emblem), treason, sedition, exposing the Blessed Sacrament under a canopy shaped like a royal cloak, devotion to the King Louis XVI, and more. Madame Lidoine held up a crucifix during the trial and said, "The only weapon we've ever had in our convent is this."[3] They were all sentenced to death though Madame Lidoine pleaded that her daughters be spared.

We are victims of our century and we must sacrifice ourselves that it be reconciled to God. An eternity of happiness awaits me. Let us hasten then, let us run toward that end and suffer willingly during the brief moments of this life. The storm rages today, but tomorrow we shall reach the harbor."[4]

—Sr. Julie Louise of Jesus
(One of the Martyrs of Compiègne)

As the sisters journeyed to their deaths at the Place de la Nation in Paris, the normally rowdy crowd was silent. At the foot of the scaffold, the sisters sang *Veni Creator Spiritus*. One of the nuns cried out, "Only too happy, O my Lord, if this little sacrifice can calm your wrath and reduce the number of victims!"[5] Madame Lidoine helped each one of the sisters up the steps to the guillotine. Hidden in the palm of her hand was a tiny statue of Mary and the child Jesus that each nun kissed as she approached her death. One by one the sisters asked for permission to die. On July 17, 1794, sixteen offerings were given to God.

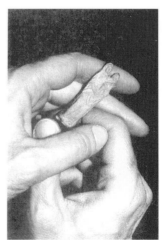

A Carmelite is one who has beheld the Crucified, who has seen him offering himself to his Father as a victim for souls and, meditating in the light of this great vision of Christ's charity, has understood the passion of love that filled his soul and has willed to give herself as he did.[6]
—Blessed Elizabeth of the Trinity

Warren Carroll, the author of *The Guillotine and the Cross*, wrote, "The Carmelite community at Compiègne had offered itself as holocaust, that peace might be restored to France and the Church. The return of full peace was still twenty-one years in the future. The Reign of Terror had only ten days left to run. Years of war, oppression and per-

Statuette kissed by the
Carmelite Martyrs

secution were yet to come, but the mass official killing in the public squares of Paris was about to end. The Cross had vanquished the Guillotine."

The Carmelites of Compiègne were beatified by Pope Pius X in 1906. Their story was the subject of a novel, *Dialogue of the Carmelites*, by Georges Bernanos and an opera by François Poulenc. In Paris, the Congregation of the Sacred Hearts of Jesus and Mary watch over their burial site at 35 rue Picpus, along with 1290 other victims of the guillotine. The tiny statue held by Madame Lidoine is preserved in the new Carmelite convent in Compiègne.

O blessed Martyrs of Compiègne,
you were offered the choice of life versus death,
and you chose life eternal.
We too are asked to make sacrifices big and small
for the sake of the Kingdom.
Help us to courageously stand with Christ no matter what the cost. Amen.

Prayer of Blessed Elizabeth of the Trinity[7]
(Elizabeth [d. 1906] was a Carmelite from Dijon)

O my God, Trinity whom I adore,
    help me forget myself entirely so to establish myself in you,
  unmovable and peaceful
    as if my soul were already in eternity.
May nothing be able to trouble my peace or make me leave you,
    O my unchanging God,
    but may each minute bring me more deeply into your mystery!
Grant my soul peace.
Make it your heaven,
    your beloved dwelling and the place of your rest.
May I never abandon you there,
    but may I be there, whole and entire,
    completely vigilant in my faith,
    entirely adoring,
    and wholly given over to your creative action. Amen.

✤ *Fifteen* ✤

John Vianney

T he little town of Ars is the final resting place of John Vianney, the Curé of Ars, who Pope Pius XI declared to be "the heavenly patron of all parish priests."[1] He hardly left the confines of his church but today he is known all around the world. Pope John Paul II said, "The Curé of Ars remains for all countries an unequaled model both of the carrying out of the ministry and the holiness of the minister."[2]

John Vianney was born in 1786 in Dardilly near Lyons. His family practiced the Catholic Faith even though the turmoil following the French Revolution resulted in the closure of their church. Priests celebrated Mass in secret and John's father often sheltered fugitive priests in their home. Early on, John learned to revere the men who risked their lives for the sake of their flocks. One biographer states, "Little did the French Revolutionaries dream that they would forge in the fire of their hate, on the anvil of their persecution, a saint who would bring back to France the very God they vowed to destroy."[3]

As a young man, John wanted nothing more than to be a priest. He was hampered by two things: his father's desire that he remain on the farm and his lack of schooling since the village school was closed. With the backing of his mother, however, John entered the minor seminary in Ecully at age nineteen under the tutelage of Father Balley.

St. John Vianney

John struggled with his classes while the younger students seem to sail along. Seeking spiritual help, he went on a pilgrimage to La Louvesc, the final resting place of St. John Francis Regis. There he prayed for the grace to learn enough Latin to make headway in his studies. From this moment on, while the road was still tortuous, John never lost heart.

There is no need for many words in order that we may pray properly. By faith we believe that there, in the sacred

Tabernacle, the good God is present. We open our hearts to Him. We rejoice that He has admitted us into His presence. This is the best method of prayer.[4]

—St. John Vianney

In 1809, John was drafted into Napoleon's army but was hospitalized due to illness. He was ordered to join his detachment which was on its way to Spain but he was unable to catch up with them. He stopped in the town of Les Noës, presented himself to the mayor and remained there in hiding, teaching children until a general amnesty was declared in 1810.

John resumed his studies with Father Balley, eventually entering the major seminary at Lyons. He flunked his examinations and returned to Father Balley. After more study, John was questioned by a board of examiners who were interviewing candidates for ordination. John was tongue-tied and confused by the questions in Latin and received an unsatisfactory assessment.

Father Balley took matters into his own hands and asked the Vicar General to grant John another chance. This time he was questioned in French in the familiar surroundings of Ecully and he did very well. Father Courbon, who was directing the diocese, asked if John was pious, had devotion to Our Lady and could say the Rosary. The answer came back that he was a model of devotion. Father Courbon said, "Very well, I will take him. The grace of God will do the rest."[5]

John was ordained in 1815 and assigned to work with Father Balley in Ecully. In 1818, he was assigned to Ars by Father Courbon who said, "There is not much love of God in that parish; you will bring some into it." Approaching Ars on foot, John asked a young boy for directions. John then said, "You have shown me the way to Ars; I will show you the way to heaven."[6] The parish was very poor, both spiritually and materially, but the mayor said upon his arrival, "We have a poor church, but a holy priest."[7]

"I will show you the way to heaven."

The Eucharist was the Curé's greatest joy. He used to call Communion un bain d'amour, *a bath of love. "Our Savior in the Holy Eucharist offers Himself each day for us to His Father's justice. If you are in difficulties and sorrows, he will relieve and comfort you. If you are sick, he will either cure you or give you the strength so as to merit heaven. If the devil, the world, and the flesh are making war upon you, he will give you weapons with which to fight, to resist and to win the victory. If you are poor, he will enrich you with all sorts of riches for time and eternity. Let us open the door of his sacred and adorable heart, and be wrapped about for an instant by the flames of his love, and we shall see what a God who loves us can do."*[8]

— St. John Vianney

When he arrived in Ars, he prayed, "Grant me the conversion of my parish, and I am ready to suffer whatever you wish for the rest of my life."[9] He spent many hours in front of the Blessed Sacrament praying for his parish while also practicing severe penances such as fasting, sleeping on boards and physical mortifications. He worried that dancing might lure his young people into immoral activities so he once intercepted a fiddler and paid him to stay away from Ars. One by one, the public houses (bars) closed. He asked workers to keep holy the Sabbath day. When people didn't come to church, he visited their homes. One Sunday, John went for a walk and saw a driverless cart. The farmer had taken cover, fearful of being seen working on the Sabbath. Father Vianney told him he should rather fear the Lord who sees everything.

Initially, John endured the scorn of some of his fellow priests. One wrote, "When a man knows as little theology as you do, he should not go into the confessional." This priest later apologized. Once a petition was circulated "accusing John of sensationalism, ignorance, and ostentatious poverty and austerities." Since "it was addressed to all the clergy, Vianney got a hold of it: Vianney read it; Vianney signed it."[10] Even though John Vianney was all too aware of his own shortcomings, the local priests later used him as their own confessor.

St. Paul tells us that when he was in Athens he found written on an altar: To the unknown God. But I, alas, might say contrary to you. I preach to you a God whom you do not adore, and whom you know to be your God. Alas! How many Christians are pressed for time, and only condescend to come for a few short moments to visit their Savior who burns with the desire to see them near Him and to tell them He loves them, and who wants to load them with blessings.[11]

—St. John Vianney

Several times John tried to leave Ars for a quiet life of prayer but he never succeeded. He often spent over sixteen hours a day in the confessional and people waited for days to see him. Two daily trains ran between Ars and Lyons to handle the crowds. There were some who were unhappy with his reforms and brought accusations against him, but an investigation exonerated him. In 1827, the Curé could say, "Ars is Ars no longer!"[12]

For many years, the devil, whom the Curé called the *Grappin* (meaning grating fork), tried to discourage John by disrupting his sleep with loud noises, setting fire to his bed and shaking the house. Witnesses testified to these disturbances. When the attacks were particularly intensive, the Curé would say, "No doubt at this moment there are some big sinners on the road to Ars!"[13] Ultimately, the attacks diminished. The Curé of Ars was the victor.

The earthly life of John Vianney came to a close on August 4, 1859. At his funeral, Abbé Beau, his confessor, said, "How many years, nay how many centuries have passed over the world, since it has seen the spectacle of a priestly life lived on such lines, so utterly and continuously dedicated and devoted, with such fruitfulness and such holiness, to the service of God? Well done, good and faithful servant."[14] In 1925, he was proclaimed St. John Vianney.

Today in Ars a new basilica holding the incorrupt body of the saint is attached to his old church. The pulpits where he preached and his old confessional can be seen. His heart, which was removed during the beatification process, is in the nearby Chapelle du Coeur. His bedroom, preserved as it was when he died, contains his bed that was singed by the devil and personal items such as his rosary, breviary and pictures.

The Curé of Ars once said, "A good pastor! A pastor who is completely obedient to the commands and wishes of Christ (is) the greatest blessing which the good God can confer on a parish."[15] God in His mercy gave not just Ars but the whole world the example of John Vianney to inspire us all.

O St. John Vianney,
you not only preached the Good News to your people,
you were a living example of Christ among us.
Help us to be holy as you strove for holiness
so that we might obtain the treasure you longed for:
life eternal, with God, forever and ever. Amen.

Prayer for Priests

O Jesus,
I pray for Your faithful and fervent priests;
for Your unfaithful and tepid priests;
for Your priests laboring at home
or abroad in distant mission fields;
for Your tempted priests;
for Your young priests;
for Your lonely and desolate priests;
for Your dying priests;
for the souls of Your priests in purgatory.

But above all I recommend to You the priests dearest to me;
the priest who baptized me;
the priest who absolved me from my sins;
the priests at whose Masses I assisted
and who gave me Your Body and Blood in Holy Communion;
the priests who taught and instructed me;
all the priests to whom I am indebted in any other way.
    O Jesus, keep them close to your heart,
        and bless them abundantly in time and eternity.
Amen.

After six years of labor, Jeanne left the hospital to recover her health and moved in with an elderly woman as her maid and companion. Jeanne lived happily there for twelve years. When her friend died, Jeanne found a roommate, Françoise Aubert, and also took in an orphan, Virginie Trédaniel. Jeanne was forty-six years old. Until now, her life was one of prayer and spiritual preparation for that "unknown work."

She loved the poor because she loved God. One day she begged her confessor to teach her how to love God even more. "Jeanne," he said, "up to now you have been giving to the poor; from now on, you must share with them."

—Paul Milcent
Jeanne Jugan: Humble So As to Love More

In 1839, many desperate and homeless people lived in Saint-Servan. One day, Jeanne carried a blind and elderly woman up the stairs to her room and gave up her bed. Shortly thereafter, another woman, who had been reduced to begging, was given Virginie's bed. Virginie and Marie Jamet, a frequent visitor, adopted a rule of life similar to the one Jeanne was following as a member of the John Eudes' apostolate.

In 1841, the little community moved to larger quarters. More poor women joined them. Within a few months, they needed larger quarters still. In 1842, Jeanne was chosen as the superior of the little group in the presence of Marie and Virginie's spiritual director, Father Le Pailleur. They called themselves the Servants of the Poor.

Jeanne was able to support their work by begging or "collecting" for their neces-

St. John Eudes is known as the father, doctor and apostle of the liturgical worship of the Hearts of Jesus and Mary for he was the first to compose a Mass and Office in their honor. He was born in Ri, Normandy, in 1601 and was ordained a priest in 1625. He was a renowned preacher and conducted over one hundred missions during his lifetime, each lasting four to six weeks. He founded two religious congregations. One was called the Congregation of Jesus and Mary (Eudists Fathers) whose mission was to educate priests (he founded six seminaries) and conduct parish missions. He also founded the Sisters of Our Lady of Charity to minister to prostitutes.

For his own congregation, John established feast days in honor of the Sacred Heart of Jesus and the Heart of Mary. John Eudes said, "Although the Heart of Jesus is distinct from that of Mary and surpasses it infinitely in excellence and holiness, yet God has so closely united these two Hearts that it may be truly said that they are but one Heart since they are always animated by the same spirit."[3] John is famous for saying that to celebrate Mass properly would take three eternities: the first to prepare for it, the second to celebrate it and the third to give thanks for it. He died in 1680 and was buried in the chapel of his seminary in Caen. After the Revolution, it was turned into a town hall and his remains were reinterred in the church of Our Lady de la Gloriette. He was canonized in 1925 on the same day as St. John Vianney.

sities. Jeanne said, "This cost me a lot to do this, but I did it for God and for our dear poor." Once she received a donation and returned to the same house the very next day. The man was not happy to see her again but she said, "But sir, my poor were hungry yesterday, they are hungry again today, and tomorrow they will be hungry, too." Another time, a man slapped her in the face and she replied, "Thank you, that was for me. Now please give me something for my poor!" She totally relied on God to provide for their needs. Monsieur Dupont, called the Holy Man of Tours, said of her work, "The finger of God is in it."[4]

At what other time and in what other way shall we be most truly children of God, can we most truly call him by his rightful name of Father, than at that moment when we consent to risk everything in absolute reliance on Him; when we believe so firmly in his love that we abandon terra firma *and cast off into the unknown, confident that the hand of God will sustain us?*[5]

—Jeanne Jugan

In 1843, her re-election as superior was unaccountably overturned by Father Le Pailleur who wanted his own choice, twenty-three-year-old Marie Jamet, in charge. Many years later Jeanne would say, "You have stolen my work from me but I willingly relinquish it to you!"[6] Jeanne continued to beg door to door. More houses were founded in Rennes, Dinan and Tours. By 1851, there were fifteen homes and three hundred sisters. But in 1852, she was recalled to the Motherhouse by Father Le Pailleur. She never again had an official public role with the Little Sisters of the Poor.

Father Le Pailleur gradually changed recorded events to make it seem as though he were the founder of the Congregation. With time, people forgot all about Jeanne. There is no record that she ever attempted to clarify the situation. She put "herself in the best possible relationship with God, and this allowed her to love more entirely; thus she found herself going backwards along the road instinctively followed by the rest of mankind." As Sister Mary of the Cross, her name in religion, there is only one recorded instance of her attending a General Council meeting where she stated that they should continue to rely on charity and not depend on investments. "To own nothing and to await all from God."[7]

We have (Jesus) in all our houses. Go and find him when your patience and strength give out and you feel alone and helpless. Jesus is waiting for you in the chapel. Say to Him: 'You know dear Jesus, what is going on. . . . You are all I have. . . . Come and help me.' And then go . . . and don't worry about how you are going to manage. He has a good memory.[8]

—Jeanne Jugan

In 1879, she died peacefully saying, "Eternal Father, open your gates today to the most wretched of your little daughters, to one, though, who longs to see you!"[9] She was buried at the Motherhouse of the Little Sisters of the Poor in Saint Pern, west of Rennes. Eventually, the true nature of Jeanne's contributions became known and Father Le Pailleur was relieved of his duties. A biographer, Cardinal Garrone, said of the last years of her life, "Renunciation of this sort, without fuss or protest, when faced with an eclipse soon to be total and to last for a quarter of a century, is truly astounding. Indeed, we have to say heroic. It is hard to imagine an equilibrium of soul capable of sustaining inner peace and serenity unaffected by such shocks. What truly human strength, what incredible resilience of character! Or to put it more precisely: what immense love!"[10]

At her beatification in 1982, Pope John Paul II stated, "In her long retirement at La Tour Saint-Joseph, many novices and Little Sisters came under her decisive influence and she left on her Congregation the stamp of her spirit by the quiet radiance of her life. In our day, pride, the pursuit of efficacy, and the temptation to use power all run rampant in the world, and sometimes, unfortunately, even in the Church. They become an obstacle to the coming of the kingdom of God. This is why the spirituality of Jeanne Jugan can attract the followers of Christ and fill their hearts with simplicity and humility, with hope and evangelical joy, having their source in God and in self-forgetfulness."[11]

O Jeanne Jugan,
where I am is where God wants me;
Too often I want to do seemingly important things
when all God wants is for me to love Him perfectly this day.
Help me to live as a true disciple of Christ
and place the outcome of all of my works in His hands. Amen.

Prayer through the Intercession of Jeanne Jugan

Jesus, you rejoiced and praised Your Father for having revealed to little ones the mysteries of the kingdom of heaven. We thank You for the graces granted to Your humble servant, Jeanne Jugan to whom we confide our petition and needs.

Father of the Poor, You have never refused the prayer of the lowly. We ask You, therefore, to hear the petitions that she presents to You on our behalf.

Jesus, through Mary, Your Mother and ours, we ask this of You, who lives and reigns with the Father and the Holy Spirit now and forever. Amen.

✤ Seventeen ✤

Catherine Labouré

The appearance of the Blessed Virgin Mary to Catherine Labouré in 1830 in the chapel of the Motherhouse of the Daughters of Charity at 140 rue du Bac in Paris ushered in the great Marian Age. It was the first in a series of apparitions culminating in Our Lady's appearance in Fatima, Portugal, in 1917. Our Lady came to warn us about evils that were about to afflict the world, but at the same time she gave us a special means by which we can receive God's grace—devotion to the Miraculous Medal. Catherine Labouré, a humble nun, was chosen to bring this powerful weapon to the world.

Catherine was born in 1806 in Fain-les-Moutiers near Dijon, the ninth child of the family. The Labourés ran a prosperous farm and Catherine was raised in a pious and happy home. When her mother died in 1815, Catherine asked the Blessed Virgin to become her mother. Her father sent her to live with relatives for awhile and, in the midst of all this change, she never attended school. When she joined the Daughters of Charity, she had to learn to read and write.

After Catherine's first Communion, she told her sister that she was going into religious life. She walked every morning to Mass in a nearby town and, as often as possible, visited the church near her home. From age fourteen on, she fasted on Fridays and Saturdays. Her sister, Tonine, said, "She was already a mystic."[1]

St. Catherine
Labouré

Suiters came to call on Catherine, but she had promised herself to Jesus. In 1824, she had an unusual dream in which an old priest beckoned her to approach him after Mass. She was frightened and ran away and instead went to visit a sick friend. The priest found her there and said, "You do well to visit the sick, my child. You flee from me now, but one day you will be glad to come to me. God has plans for you; do not forget it!"[2]

Catherine's father, to her dismay, did not give her permission to enter religious life. Instead, he sent her to Paris to work in her brother's restaurant. Her sister-in-law rescued her and brought her to live with them at Châtillon-sur-Seine. One day, Catherine visited the nearby convent of the Daughters of Charity and was surprised to see a picture of the old priest from the dream in the parlor. When she asked whose picture it was, the reply came, "This is our founder, St. Vincent de Paul."[3] Convinced that this was where God wanted her, Catherine was able to gain her father's permission to enter religious life.

Upon her arrival at the Motherhouse, Catherine was part of a procession that accompanied the remains of Vincent de Paul to a church on the rue de Sévres. During the Revolution, his remains were hidden to protect them from destruction. After the ceremony, the heart of Vincent appeared to Catherine in three different ways, foretelling of peace and renewal for the community and the fall of the French king.

During her novitiate, Catherine was able to see Jesus truly present in the Blessed Sacrament and, one time, Jesus as Christ the King. "I saw Him during the whole time of my seminary, except when I doubted; the next time, I saw nothing, because I had wished to penetrate the mystery, and believing myself deceived, had doubted."[4]

On July 18, 1830, on the eve of the feast of St. Vincent de Paul, Catherine was awakened by a radiant child who said, "Come with me to the chapel; the Blessed Virgin awaits you!" The chapel was ablaze with candlelight and torches, reminding Catherine of midnight Mass, and the child said, "Here is the Blessed Virgin; here she is!" A beautiful lady bowed before the tabernacle and seated herself in a chair. Catherine went down on her knees and rested her hands on Mary's lap. Our Lady

The Blessed Mother's appearances at La Salette (1846) and Lourdes (1858) were followed by others at Pontmain and Pellevoisin. In 1871, during the Franco-Prussian War, the Blessed Virgin Mary appeared in Pontmain, a town south east of Mont Saint-Michel. The Prussians were in the nearby town of Laval and Pontmain had sent thirty-eight of its men to fight in the war. On the evening of January 17, Mary appeared to four children. The priest, though he could not see the apparition, led the village in prayer. In the night sky, these words became visible, "Pray, my children, God will answer you in a short while. My Son will let himself be moved."[5] Then a red crucifix appeared with the words *Jesus Christ* written on it. After two hours, the apparition ceased. The next day, the Prussians inexplicably retreated and the war was over within two weeks.

In 1876, Our Lady appeared fifteen times to Estelle Faguette, a thirty-two-year-old servant girl from Pellevoisin near Châteauroux. Estelle was near death with tuberculosis. Mary told her that she would suffer for five more days in honor of Jesus' five wounds and, if she were cured, she should publicly glorify God. Mary also said, "What afflicts me most is the want of respect shown by some people to my divine Son in Holy Communion and the attitude taken in prayer, when at the same time the mind continues occupied with other things."[6] Estelle was totally cured and lived another fifty-three years.

said, "God wishes to entrust you with a mission." It would be a cause of great suffering for her. "Great misfortune will come to France" and the Archbishop himself would die, but God and St. Vincent would protect their community. "But come to the foot of this altar where great grace awaits all, whether they be great or little, who ask fervently and with confidence."[7]

In truth, what is Mary's maternal mediation if not the Father's gift to humanity?[8]
—Pope John Paul II

The second apparition occurred in the same chapel on November 27, 1830. Catherine saw the Blessed Virgin standing on a globe, her feet resting on a serpent (Gn 3:15) and around her head twelve stars ("A great sign appeared in the sky, a woman clothed with the sun, with the moon under her feet and on her head a crown of twelve stars" [Rev 12:1]). In her hands Mary held a golden ball with a cross on top that represented the world and all people, especially France. On her fingers were rings, set with gems, that radiated rays of light. The rays were the graces bestowed on those who asked for them. The gems that did not radiate light were the graces for which she was not asked. When Our Lady stretched out her arms, showering graces down on the world, the words: "O Mary, conceived without sin, pray for us who have recourse to thee" appeared in a semi-circle over her head. The image turned and on the back was a large "M" topped by a cross and underneath two hearts: Mary's pierced by a sword and Jesus' crowned with thorns. Twelve stars encircled this vision. Our Lady told Catherine to have this image struck into a medal.

The remaining years of Catherine's life were devoted to this mission. She told no one about the revelations except her confessor, Father Aladel. He doubted her at first but after her repeated pleas, conveyed Our Lady's request to the Archbishop of Paris and, in 1832, the first medal was issued. Within four years, over ten million medals were distributed.

Those who wear this medal around their neck with confidence will receive great graces.[9]

—Our Lady to Catherine Labouré

The most famous story about the power of the Miraculous Medal is the conversion of Alphonse Ratisbonne. A Jewish man by birth, he was an atheist who happened to be visiting Rome. He was asked by a devout gentleman to wear the medal and say the *Memorarae*. Much to his surprise, he couldn't get the prayer off of his mind. In the Church of San' Andrea delle Fratte, the Blessed Virgin appeared to him and he instantly believed. He became a Catholic priest with the Fathers of Sion, founded by his brother Theodore. He is buried outside of Jerusalem in Ein Karem under a statue of Mary. His tombstone reads, "O Mary, remember your child who is the sweet and glorious conquest of your love."

Let us contribute all our strength in bringing about what was already foreseen by St. Catherine Labouré, to whom the Immaculata graciously revealed the Miraculous Medal, that the Immaculata be queen of the whole world and of each soul in particular as soon as possible.[10]

—St. Maximilian Kolbe

During her life, no one, not even her superior, knew that she was the recipient of the revelations of the Miraculous Medal. She spent the next forty-six years at Enghien, outside Paris, where she cared for elderly men. Late in her life, distressed because a statue requested by the Blessed Virgin had not been erected in the chapel, she told the truth about the apparition to her superior, Mother Dufes, who got the work underway. Catherine died in 1876 and her incorrupt body rests today in chapel of the Motherhouse of the Daughters of Charity under the statue of Our Lady of the Globe. Catherine was canonized in 1946 by Pope Pius XII as the "Saint of Silence."

The words of Pope Pius XII from her canonization sum up the character of Catherine: "Impelled by the urging of love, she hurried eagerly before the tabernacle as often as she could, or before the sacred image of her holy Mother, to pour out the desires of her heart and to make an offering of the fragrance of her prayers. Accordingly, it was evident that, while she dwelt in earthly exile, in mind and heart she lived in heaven."[11]

O Catherine Labouré,
you were graced with heavenly visions,
yet in your lifetime you were unknown to the world.
Help me to realize that God is asking me to do
the little things in life, unseen by the world, with the same devotion;
that the road to my saintliness
is how I live my life each day. Amen.

Act of Consecration
to Our Lady of the Miraculous Medal

Virgin Mother of God, Mary Immaculate,
we dedicate and consecrate ourselves to you
  under the title of Our Lady of the Miraculous Medal.
May this medal be for each of us a sure sign
  of your affection for us
  and a constant reminder of our duties towards you.
Ever while wearing it, may we be blessed by your loving protection
  and preserved in the grace of your Son.
Most powerful Virgin, Mother of our Savior,
  keep us close to you every moment of our lives.
Obtain for us, your children, the grace of a happy death,
  so that, in union with you, we may enjoy the
  happiness of heaven forever. Amen.

✤ *Eighteen* ✤

Peter Julian Eymard

S t. Peter Julian Eymard is called the Apostle of the Eucharist because he sought to rekindle in the world a greater love for Jesus, present Body, Blood, Soul and Divinity in the Holy Eucharist. In France, during the nineteenth century, reception of Communion was infrequent and many churches were empty or locked throughout the day. He saw devotion to the Blessed Sacrament as important "not only for personal piety, (but) essential to social life, for it is the very life of the world."[1]

> *The life of St. Peter Julian Eymard, the standard-bearer, herald and champion of Christ's presence in the sacred tabernacle, is, like that of the Baptist, a shining and burning light . . . through which the ancient Secret of the Eucharist was revealed to the world.*[2]
>
> —Pope Pius XII

Peter Julian was born in 1811 at La Mure d'Isére, near Grenoble, into a large and loving family. Thanks to his mother's example, he loved the Blessed Sacrament and often visited Jesus saying, "a friend would never pass by his friend without saying a word to him. Well, I must often visit my Beloved."[3] After his first Communion, he promised the Lord that he would become a

St. Peter Julian Eymard

priest. But death robbed Peter Julian of all of his brothers and sisters except one and his father wanted him to remain in the family business. Leaving school at age thirteen, he studied Latin in secret, finally gaining his father's approval to enter the Oblates of Mary in 1829. His stay was short. Due to his own grave illness, he returned home. After the death of his father, he entered the Grenoble Seminary where he was ordained a priest in 1834.

Peter Julian was only in a parish for a few years but his dedication was remembered long afterwards. His parishioners recalled that he typically arrived at the church early in

Incorrupt body of Peter Julian Eymard

the morning, celebrated Mass and then remained prostrate in front of the Blessed Sacrament for a long time where he composed his sermons. His day ended with another visit to Jesus and the recitation of the Stations of the Cross. When he felt a calling to join the Society of Mary, or Marists, his parishioners petitioned the bishop. While touched by their love for him, Peter Julian had to remain faithful to his call; the Lord wanted him elsewhere.

As a Marist, Peter Julian became provincial and also superior of a college but he was not so renowned that he forgot the poor. When civil unrest broke out, Peter Julian was grabbed by a mob and almost thrown into a river but someone said, "No, no, not him! He is a friend of the workers!"[4] After seventeen years as a Marist, Peter Julian felt another call "to bring all the world to the knowledge and love of our Lord; to preach nothing else but Jesus Christ and Jesus Christ Eucharistic."[5] He was given a choice: abandon this Eucharistic project or leave the Marists. He said, "I see that God is requiring of me to make a complete break, that I must even burn my bridges behind me. The sacrifice must be total. God is demanding full abandonment to His grace."[6]

In a letter to St. John Vianney, Father Eymard wrote that the purpose of this new society was "to make Jesus in the Blessed Sacrament known, loved, and served by all hearts. It aims to form for Him a court of faithful adorers and a guard of honor always watching in His presence." Their mission would be contemplative but also active, "searching out, and preparing for First Communion those who did not have the joy of doing so when they were young."[7]

While seeking people to join his new order, he also supported lay organizations that promoted adoration. Speaking in Brussels in 1858, he said, "It is a sad thing to admit, but if timid, fearful and diffident people are to be found on the face of the earth, they are Catholics. . . . Will you remain cold and indifferent? No! If there are societies for the spreading of evil, you will form a society for the spreading of good, a society of adoration. . . . And how often have I repeated it, nothing short of perpetual adoration will start a conflagration. . . . Never should Our Lord find Himself alone here."[8]

Pope John XXII, preaching one day on the Eucharistic heaven of Jesus, said that holy souls began their heaven around the Blessed Sacrament in the parish where they died, in order to be part of the court of Jesus, and that they could stay as long as Jesus did. That thought has often consoled me. I like to go and pray in the church of the parish where my parents died, because of this pleasing and consoling thought.[9]

—Peter Julian Eymard

The road was not easy for Peter Julian. He suffered from migraines, rheumatism, bronchitis, shingles and heart problems. The congregation he founded, the Congregation of the Blessed Sacrament (SSS) and the Servants of the Blessed Sacrament, a cloistered contemplative order of women he co-founded with Marguerite Guillot, had few vocations initially. Near the end of his life he was publicly humiliated. Human consolation was often absent. He accepted this, "suffering in his own body the pains of Him who hung on the Cross."[10]

Devotion that has not a tent on Calvary and one near the tabernacle, will not result in solid piety and will never accomplish anything great. I find that we do not preach enough on this Mystery of Love par excellence. As a result, souls suffer, become sensual and material in their piety, and are inordinately attached to creatures because they fail to find their consolation and strength in our Lord.[11]

—Peter Julian Eymard

Peter Julian died in 1868 at La Mure. His sister wanted his body to remain there but after her death, his body was reinterred in Paris in the Chapelle du Saint Sacrement at 23 avenue de Friedland. Today, the Blessed Sacrament religious have more than one hundred foundations around the world. With their encouragement, the first Eucharistic Congress was held in France in 1874. Today, many churches have opened their doors for Eucharistic adoration, for there, as Peter Julian said, "is a remedy for our spiritual infirmities, strength for our daily weaknesses, and a source of peace, joy and happiness."[12]

Peter Julian was canonized in 1962 at the end of the first session of the Second Vatican Council. Pope John XXIII said, "Next to a St. Vincent de Paul, a St. John Eudes, a Curé of Ars, Peter Julian Eymard takes his place today among the ranks of shining luminaries who are the glory and honor of their country, which gave them birth, but whose blessed influence extends far beyond into the entire Church. His characteristic mark, the guiding thought all of his priestly activities, we can say, was the Eucharist: the worship and mission of the Eucharist."[13]

O Peter Julian Eymard,
you heard the call of the Lord
and never wavered in carrying out His work in the world.
Following your example,
let us often place ourselves
before the Lord in the Blessed Sacrament
so that the voice we hear and respond to
is the Lord's and no other. Amen.

To Our Lady of the Most Blessed Sacrament

(St. Peter Julian Eymard called Mary Our Lady of the Blessed Sacrament)

As I kneel here in the presence of your Son, Jesus,
my thoughts turn to you, His Mother,
   under the title of Our Lady of the Most Blessed Sacrament,
   and I address to you my prayer of strong faith
   and fervent petition:
   Virgin Immaculate, Mother of Jesus and my Mother,
   I invoke you under the title
   of Our Lady of the Most Blessed Sacrament,
   because you are the Mother of the Savior
   who lives in the Eucharist.
It was from you that He took flesh and blood
   which He feeds me in the sacred Host.
I also invoke you under the title because
   the grace of the Eucharist comes to me through you,
   since you are the mediatrix, the channel
   through which God's graces reach me.
And finally, I call you
   Our Lady of the Most Blessed Sacrament
   because you were the first to live the Eucharistic life.
Teach me to pray the Mass as you did,
   to receive Holy Communion worthily and frequently,
   and to visit devoutly with your Son, Jesus,
   in the Blessed Sacrament. Amen.

✢ *Nineteen* ✢

Notre Dame des Victoires

Paris has many beautiful and historic churches and among them is Our Lady of Victories or Notre Dame des Victoires. It was at one time a popular pilgrimage destination but in the dismal days following the French Revolution, it was just another poorly attended church. Notre Dame des Victoires' revival was sparked by one man who turned his parish over to the Mother of God.

The first church erected on the site, administered by the Augustinian friars, was built in 1590 and dedicated to Our Lady. In 1619, they acquired a statue called Our Lady of Montaigu and it became a popular pilgrimage site. King Louis XIII promised to build a larger church on the condition that it be named Our Lady of Victories in thanksgiving for a great military victory over the Protestants at La Rochelle. Construction began in 1629.

During the French Revolution, the church was closed and ultimately became a stock exchange. In 1809, it was restored to a church but it languished because in the intervening years, many people had abandoned their faith and no longer came to Mass.

On December 3, 1836, the parish priest, Father des Genettes, was discouraged and ready to resign. While celebrating Mass one day, distracted and disturbed that his efforts seemed to bear no fruit, he heard a voice say, "Consecrate your parish to the Most Holy and Immaculate Heart of Mary." After Mass ended, he wondered if he was imagining things but he heard again, "Consecrate your parish to the Most Holy and Immaculate Heart of Mary."[1]

Our Lady of Victories

He immediately composed guidelines for a confraternity that the bishop approved within the same week. During Mass on the following Sunday, he told the ten people in attendance that vespers would be held in the evening and the rules of this new confraternity would be spelled out. That evening, the church was full. Miracles attributed to Our Lady's intercession occurred almost immediately and were commemorated with plaques on the walls of the church.

Two years later, Pope Gregory XVI named the organization the Archconfraternity of the Holy and Immaculate Heart of Mary for the Conversion of Sinners. Fr. Pierre De Smet, a Belgian Jesuit missionary to North America, visited Notre Dame des Victoires in 1847 and enrolled some of the newly converted American Indians into the Archconfraternity.

In 1854, the dogma of the Immaculate Conception was proclaimed: "The Most Blessed Virgin Mary was from the first moment of her conception, by a singular grace and privilege of almighty God and by virtue of the merits of Jesus Christ, Savior of the human race, preserved immune from all stain of original sin."[2] Prayers of thanksgiving were said at Notre Dame des Victoires and people saw the statue of the Immaculate Heart of Mary move. Pope Pius IX had the statue crowned in 1856 and Pope Pius XI raised the church to a minor basilica.

The title given to Mary as Our Lady of Victory is associated with one of the most significant battles ever fought in history. The Moslem Turks were attacking cities in the Mediterranean and were threatening Italy. Responding to Pope Pius V's call for help, a fleet of ships supplied by the Italian states and Spain were placed under the leadership of Don Juan of Austria. Meanwhile, the Rosary Confraternity of Rome prayed for Our Lady's intercession. On October 7, 1571, the Christian forces defeated the Ottoman Turks in the Battle of Lepanto. To commemorate the victory, the Dominican Pope, St. Pius V, established October 7 as a feast day called Our Lady of Victory. Today it is known as the feast of Our Lady of the Most Holy Rosary.

St. Thérèse of Lisieux had a great love for Notre Dame des Victoires. When she was very ill as a young girl, her father had Masses said for her recovery at the church. When she visited Paris on her way to Rome in 1887, only one sight filled her with delight as she related in *Story of a Soul*, Our Lady of Victories! "Ah, what I felt kneeling at her feet cannot be expressed. The graces she granted me so moved me that my happiness found expression only in tears, just as on the day of my First Communion. The Blessed Virgin made me feel it was really herself who smiled on me and brought about my cure."

Fr. Hermann Cohen, a Jewish convert, was in another church when he observed some lay women praying in front of the Blessed Sacrament with the intent of staying all night long. Monsignor, later Bishop, de la Bouillerie told him to "round up some men and women and we will authorize you to imitate the devout women whose privilege you so envy."[3] Hermann and his volunteers met for the first time at Notre Dame des Victoires in 1848 and formed the Nocturnal Adoration Society. Membership quickly increased and the Society spread around the world.

In 1842, Fr. Theodore Ratisbonne, a Jewish convert to Catholicism, announced at Notre Dame des Victoires that his brother Alphonse had become a "fully believing Catholic" after the Blessed Virgin Mary appeared to him in Rome. Theodore had asked the Arch-confraternity to pray for his brother during his journey. Theodore, born into a Jewish family in Strasbourg in 1802, was baptized in 1827 and ordained a priest in 1830. He founded the Congregation of Our Lady of Sion in 1848. Near the end of his life he said, "Death, properly so-called, does not exist for a soul nourished by the Living Bread from heaven, so what we should fear least of all is death."[4]

Hermann Cohen, founder of the Nocturnal Adoration Society, was born into a Jewish family in Hamburg, Germany, in 1821. When he was asked to direct a choir in the church of St. Valeria in Paris, he became captivated by the Catholic Church after seeing the monstrance raised during exposition of the Blessed Sacrament. Hermann was baptized in Fr. Theodore Ratisbonne's chapel in 1847 and was ordained a Carmelite priest in 1851. To his niece he wrote, "I have retired into the deep solitude of the desert, so that I may spend my days and nights in unceasing colloquies with our Lord in the Blessed Eucharist . . . where I have never experienced a moment of weariness or lassitude."[5] He died in Germany in 1871 of smallpox contracted from French prisoners-of-war.

Theodore and Alphonse Ratisbonne

There is a link between Notre Dame des Victoires and the apparition of the Blessed Virgin at Pontmain in 1871. At the very moment when Our Lady was appearing in Pontmain and the Prussians were besieging France, Father Amodru spoke at Notre Dame des Victoires and proclaimed, "We are all going to publicly and solemnly beg the most Blessed Virgin to come to our aid and we will not cross the threshold of this holy temple consecrated to her glory without solemnly promising to offer her a silver heart, which will recall to future generations that today, between eight and nine o'clock in the evening, an entire nation is prostrated at the feet of Our Lady of Victories and has been saved by her."[6] An armistice was signed between France and Germany eleven days later ending the Franco-Prussian War.

St. John Bosco made Notre Dame des Victoires the first church he visited in Paris in 1883. He was scheduled to celebrate Mass at nine in the morning but by seven the church was full. When someone expressed surprise at the crowd, a woman said, "You see, it is the Mass for sinners, and it is going to be said by a saint."[7]

Notre Dame des Victoires is still a center for pilgrimage and adoration. The Benedictine Sisters of Montmartre Sacré-Coeur look after the Basilica. One of the windows honors Father des Genettes who consecrated his parish to the Immaculate Heart of Mary. His act of faith brought about the conversion of his parish and established an important place of prayer in the midst of a grand city.

Our Lady of Victory,
war and strife are ever present today
and indeed they are yokes
we pass on from generation to generation.
May we remember that true peace only comes from your Son.
May we be channels of His peace. Amen.

Excerpt of a Meditation by Hermann Cohen [8]

Jesus, let me tell you what you are to my soul.
Today I am weak;
   I need a strength from on high to sustain me;
   and Jesus descended from Heaven;
   Jesus has become the Eucharist, the Bread of the strong!

Today I am poor!
In need of shelter, and Jesus makes Himself my home.
This is the House of God, the Gate of Heaven, the Eucharist.

Today I am hungry and thirsty;
   I need a nourishment which will satisfy my mind and heart,
   a beverage to quench my thirst:
   and Jesus becomes the Eucharistic Wheat and Wine.

Today I am suffering;
   I need a beneficent balsam to heal the wounds of my soul;
   and Jesus in the Holy Eucharist is the precious balm
   poured forth upon them.

Today I want to offer to God a Holocaust pleasing to Him;
   and Jesus makes Himself the Victim;
   Jesus in the Eucharist.

✣ Twenty ✣
Our Lady of La Salette

France has been blessed with many saints throughout the centuries but has also struggled to keep a Christian identity. In the mid-nineteenth century, in the years following the French Revolution, church attendance was down, the Sacraments were neglected and secularism prevailed. Into this world the Blessed Mother came to awaken her children.

Taken up to heaven, Mary did not lay aside this saving office, but by her manifold intercession she continues to bring us the gifts of eternal salvation. By her maternal charity, she cares for the brethren of her Son, who still journey on earth surrounded by dangers and difficulties, until they are led into the happiness of their true home.[1]
—*Lumen Gentium*

On September 9, 1846, on the eve of the feast of Our Lady of Sorrows, Mélanie Calvat (age 14) and Maximin Giraud (age 11), who had met two

Our Lady of La Salette

days earlier, were tending their cows high in the mountains of the French Alps. They dozed off after lunch and awoke to find their cows missing. They quickly found them and when Mélanie turned back to gather their belongings, she saw a globe of fire "like the sun had fallen there."[2] She called to Maximin who said he would give it a good whack if it came too close. The circle opened to reveal a woman sitting with her hands over her face. She was weeping, as if consumed with grief.

Wearing a white dress and yellow apron, she was bathed in light. A large luminous crucifix containing a hammer and tongs hung on a chain around her neck. Another chain ringed her shawl. A crown, surrounded with roses, rested on her head. Her shawl and shoes were also ringed with roses. The lady told them not to be afraid, that she had great news to tell them.

"If my people will not obey, I shall be compelled to loose my Son's arm. It is so heavy, so pressing that I can no longer restrain it. How long I have suffered for you! If my Son is not to cast you off, I am obliged to entreat Him without ceasing."

"I have appointed you six days for working. The seventh I have reserved for myself. And no one will give it to me. . . . The cart drivers cannot swear without bringing in my Son's name. These are two things which make my Son's arm so burdensome."

The crucifix worn by Our Lady of La Salette is rich in symbolism. The hammer symbolizes our sins which were driven as nails into our Lord's hands and feet during the crucifixion. The tongs or pliers remove these nails or sins and symbolize our reconciliation with God. Mary wept over the sins of God's people during the apparition. The La Salette missionaries work to bring God's mercy and forgiveness to all the world, lightening the arm of the Lord that weighs so heavily on His mother.

"If the harvest is spoiled, it is your own fault. I warned you last year by means of the potatoes. You paid no heed. Quite the reverse, when you discovered that the potatoes had rotted, you swore, you abused my Son's name."

The lady spoke to them in French but Mélanie did not understand the word "pommes de terre" or potato, so the lady switched to the local dialect. "A great famine is coming. But before that happens, the children under seven years of age will be seized with trembling and die in their parents arms. The grownups will pay for their sins by hunger. The grapes will rot and the walnuts will turn bad."

She then confided a secret to each of the children. "If people are converted, the rocks will become piles of wheat, and it will be found that the potatoes have sown themselves."

She asked if the children said their prayers and when they answered hardly at all, she said to say morning and evening prayers or at least a Hail Mary and an Our Father every day. "Only a few rather old women go to Mass in the summer. All the rest work every Sunday throughout the summer. And in winter, when they don't know what to do with themselves, they go to Mass only to poke fun at religion. During Lent, they flock to the butcher shops, like dogs."

She then told Maximin about an incident known only to him and his father. Speaking again in French, she ended with these words, "My children you will make this known to all my people. You will make this known to all my people."[3]

The lady rose into the air, looked up to heaven with her face now joyful and disappeared. When they returned to the town of Les Ablandins that evening, Maximin told Mélanie's employers what had occurred. The grand-

Mélanie and Maximin have not been declared saints but still the Church recognizes their revelations as authentic. Neither of them would find peace on earth. Both of them were born in Corps, the town at the base of the road that leads to La Salette. Mélanie was born in 1831. Her father was often gone and her mother did not care for her. Mélanie was farmed out as a shepherdess and was often abused by her employers. It was only after the apparition that she was instructed in the Faith and received her first Communion. She attempted to enter religious life several times unsuccessfully. She died alone in 1904 in Altamura, Italy. When a priest asked her if she ever tired of talking about the apparition, she said, "No, sir, do you get tired of saying Mass over and over?"

Maximin too had a difficult life. His mother died when he was young and his stepmother abused him. He wanted to become a priest but was a poor student. He tried various occupations and eventually joined the Papal Zouaves, soldiers for the Pope, for awhile. He died at age thirty-nine and said of his life, "The Blessed Virgin wanted me just as I am."[4]

Mélanie Calvat

mother exclaimed, "It is the Virgin that these children have seen. She is the only one whose Son reigns in heaven."[5] The first priest to hear about the apparition, Jacques Perrin, founded a confraternity and asked the members to recite the following prayer every day, "Our Lady of La Salette, reconciler of sinners, pray without ceasing for those who have recourse to thee."

Having invoked the Holy Spirit and the help of the Immaculate Virgin, (we have concluded that the apparition) bears all of the characteristics of truth and the faithful have grounds for believing it indubitable and with certainty. Reexamine yourselves seriously, do penance for your sins. Become submissive to the voice of Mary calling you to penance and who, on behalf of her Son, threatens you with spiritual and temporal ills, if remaining insensitive to her maternal admonitions, you should harden your hearts.[6]
—Bishop de Bruillard

After the apparition, the people of the area returned to the Sacraments in large numbers, including Maximin's father. Numerous cures were attributed to Our Lady of La Salette's intercession, including miracles associated with a spring that began to flow steadily at the apparition site. To support the pilgrims and to spread the message given at La Salette, a new community of priests and brothers was established: "Moved by the Holy Spirit who prompted the Son of God to experience our human condition and die on the cross in order to reconcile the world to the Father, we resolve, in the light of the apparition of Our Lady of La Salette, to be devoted servants of Christ and of the Church for the fulfillment of the mystery of reconciliation."[7]

Maximin and Mélanie both tried to enter religious life but were unsuccessful. It is tempting to look at their struggles in life and pass judgment on the apparition as well. Whatever their faults, they never changed their testimony and were faithful to the mission entrusted to them. As Maximin said, "The apparition has not changed us, it has left us with all of our faults."[8]

St. John Vianney did not initially believe in the apparition but became a supporter after a specific favor was granted to him through Our Lady of La Salette. He said, "I tell you, one can and one must believe in La Salette."[9] St. Peter Julian Eymard wrote in a visitor's log in 1852, "If I did not have the good fortune to be a Marist, I would ask my bishop, as a special favor, to dedicate myself body and soul to the service of Our Lady of La Salette."[10]

I believe firmly in, and will defend to the last drop of my blood, the celebrated apparition of the most Blessed Virgin on the mountain of La Salette, on September 19, 1846, an apparition to which I have testified by my own words in writing and in suffering.[11]

—Maximin's Last Will and Testament

A beautiful shrine was built near the site of the apparition, and today, a guest house provides pilgrims with a place for prayer and self-reflection in the solitude of the mountains. Statues mark where the significant events took place. Meanwhile, the work of the La Salette missionaries goes on around the world. As the Bishop of Grenoble stated, "The mission of the two shepherds has come to an end, that of the Church now begins."[12]

Dear Lady of La Salette,
your Son sent you from heaven
to warn us of the consequences of disobedience to the Father.
You call each of us to reform our lives.
Help us to do so.
And at the end of our days,
may we be united with Jesus forever in heaven. Amen.

Memorarae of Our Lady of La Salette

Remember, Our Lady of La Salette,
true Mother of Sorrows,
  the tears you shed for me on Calvary.
Remember also the care you have always taken
  to keep me faithful to Christ your Son.
After having done so much for your child,
  you will not abandon me now.
Inspired by this consoling thought,
  I come to cast myself at your feet
  in spite of my infidelities and ingratitude.
Do not reject my prayer, O merciful Virgin,
  but intercede for my conversion.
Obtain for me the grace to love Jesus above all things,
  and to console you by a holy life,
  that I may one day see you in heaven. Amen.

❧ Twenty-one ❧
Our Lady of Lourdes

In 1862, the Lourdes Commission issued the following statement: "We hold that the Immaculate Mary, Mother of God, actually appeared to Bernadette Soubirous on the eleventh of February 1858, and on the days following, to the number of eighteen times, in the grotto of Massabielle, near the town of Lourdes. That this apparition bears all the signs of authenticity and that the faithful are free to consider it true."[1]

Thus, the Church proclaimed what many people already believed to be true; the Mother of God did appear to Bernadette Soubirous at the grotto of Massabielle. Perhaps no other apparition site has captured the hearts of people like Lourdes. It is a place of hope, love and healing, and for those seeking restoration of body, mind or spirit, one cannot leave Lourdes without being touched in some profound way.

Bernadette Soubirous was born in Lourdes in 1844, in the shadows of the Pyrénées mountains, to François and Louise Soubirous. They were a poor family and, at one point, François was falsely accused of stealing flour for his family and was arrested. Bernadette was a sickly child who suffered from asthma, aggravated by the poor food and living conditions the family endured. Their home was appropriately named the *Cachot*, or the dungeon, because it was once a jail.

St. Bernadette Soubirous

On February 11, 1858, Bernadette was collecting firewood with her sister and a friend near the River Gave. Bernadette remained behind to remove her stockings while the other two crossed the icy river. There was a gust of wind and when Bernadette looked up, she saw a "beautiful girl" in the niche above a cave which was called the Grotto of Massabielle ("old rock"). The lady was dressed in a white robe with a blue sash around her waist. A white rosary, linked with a gold chain that shone like the yellow roses on her feet, rested on her arm. As the lady, whom

Bernadette called *Aquero* (That one), made the sign of the cross, Bernadette did the same. Together they prayed the rosary, the Lady silently passing the beads through her fingers, then the apparition ended.

Bernadette told her sister what she had seen and the news spread quickly. Her mother thought that she had deceived herself and Bernadette had to wait for three days before her family would allow her to return to the Grotto. When the Lady appeared again, Bernadette sprinkled holy water on her and asked if she came from God or from somewhere else. The lady did not reply. Bernadette seemed to be in ecstasy and, when people tried to move her, she did not budge.

> *Bernadette celebrated her First Communion in June 1858, a few months after the first apparition. When asked what made her happier, receiving Jesus in the Holy Eucharist or seeing Our Lady, she said, "Those are two things which go together, but cannot be compared. Both made me very happy."[2]*
>
> —St. Bernadette

During the third apparition, the lady asked Bernadette to come back to the Grotto for fifteen days and told her, "I do not promise to make you happy in this world, but in the next."[3] As the apparitions continued, the crowds grew, even though nothing could be seen by the people. After the sixth apparition, the authorities questioned her and accused her of lying. Bernadette's simple answers confounded them.

During the eighth apparition, the Lady said, "Penance," and told Bernadette to pray for the conversion of sinners. During the next apparition she was told to drink from a spring and wash in it. She did not see a spring and started to go to the river but the Lady pointed to muddy water under a rock which Bernadette drank and spread over her face. Bernadette also gathered some leaves from a wild plant and ate them. People thought that she might be crazy. But after Bernadette left, the mud turned into a clear stream of water and people began to drink and bottle it.

> *To eat grass and drink muddy water from Bernadette's cupped hands was to show to what extent sin had humiliated humanity. When we sin we are no different than the beasts of the field. Penance opens up our eyes not only to our sinfulness but to the dignity to which each one of us is called and created by God.*
>
> —Fr. Patrick Greenough, OFM CONV.
> *Immaculata* Magazine

During the thirteenth apparition, the Lady asked that a chapel be built and processions be conducted. For the first time, Bernadette approached

The Grotto of Massabielle

Father Peyramale, the parish priest of Lourdes. He was impressed with Bernadette's sincerity and saw firsthand that there was an increase in attendance at Lenten services and confession. However, this was a girl who hardly knew her catechism. And the identity of the Lady was unknown. He dismissed her and waited.

During the sixteenth apparition, on the feast of the Annunciation, the Lady revealed who she was, saying, "I am the Immaculate Conception." The dogma of the Immaculate Conception had been proclaimed by Pope Pius IX four years before in 1854, but Bernadette had never heard of it. When she understood what it meant, it confirmed what people already suspected; the Lady really was the Blessed Virgin.

Miracles of healing occurred almost immediately at the Grotto and a fence was put up to stop the flood of pilgrims. But the people kept coming. The medical archives at Lourdes contain over five thousand cases of healing, many during the Blessed Sacrament procession. One of the most famous is the story of John Traynor from England. John was wounded during World War I and left with a paralyzed arm, partially paralyzed legs and epilepsy. In 1923, he traveled to Lourdes even though he was told that he might die if he made the trip. He bathed in the waters and was cured of his seizures but was still a very sick man. During the procession of the Blessed Sacrament, a bishop stopped in front of him with the monstrance and blessed him. His arm, which had been useless, began to move. His caretakers gave him a sedative not believing he was cured, only upset and agitated. The next morning, he ran to the Grotto. He had been unable to stand or walk for eight years. According to the Medical Bureau, "this extraordinary cure is absolutely beyond and above the powers of nature."[4]

At Lourdes, even Mary has stepped aside to make way for Christ. There is no place in the world where Christ in the Eucharist is more glorified. The procession of the Eucharist by candlelight is the high point of each day. Here the pilgrims are joined in faith, and all the countries of the world are united as the procession winds from the grotto to show that Jesus is the Gift of the Virgin Mary. Now she stands at the side of her Son so that He may console.

—Rev. Msgr. John F. Davis
An Audience with Jesus

Bernadette became a sister of Notre Dame of Nevers in 1866. Father Peyramale told her, "Your mission at the Grotto is finished; work for your sanctification; live a life hidden in Jesus Christ, show God how grateful you are for all of the favors he has accorded you by living an exemplary life in the holy house that has welcomed you."[5] She died in 1879, never to see again her beloved Grotto. "I gave up Lourdes," she said, "I'll see the Blessed Virgin in heaven; it will be much more beautiful."[6]

The unique glory of the shrine of Lourdes resides in the fact that Mary attracts to it people from everywhere for the adoration of Jesus Christ in the Blessed Sacrament, so that this sanctuary, which is at the same time the center of Marian devotion and the throne of Eucharistic mystery, seems to surpass in glory all others of the Catholic Church.[7]

—Pope Pius X

Today, pilgrims still bathe in the waters at the Grotto and participate in the procession of the Blessed Sacrament. It is also possible to visit Bernadette's birthplace, her home and see the font where she was baptized. Millions of pilgrims come to Lourdes every year to seek healing and to experience an inexplicable closeness to God.

Through the intercession of the Blessed Virgin,
I ask You Lord Jesus to hear my prayer.
Heal me this day of anything
that is an obstacle to uniting myself with You.
Dear Blessed Mother, intercede for me,
for your Son cannot refuse your request. Amen.

Prayer to Our Lady of Lourdes

 ever Immaculate Virgin Mother of mercy,
Health of the sick,
Refuge of sinners,
Comfort of the afflicted,
you know my wants, my troubles, my sufferings,
deign to cast upon me a look of mercy.

By appearing at the Grotto of Lourdes,
you were pleased to make it a privileged sanctuary,
where you dispense your favors;
and already many sufferers have obtained
the cure of their infirmities,
both spiritual and corporal.

I come, therefore, with the most unbounded confidence
to implore your maternal intercession.
Obtain, O loving Mother, the granting of my requests.

Through gratitude for favors,
I will endeavor to imitate your virtues,
that one day I may share your glory. Amen.

those Masses especially during my sleepless nights."[2]

She had hoped that her life in the convent would free her from the burden of speaking to those who were curious to see her—but the visits continued. She made no secret of the fact that she did not like being gawked at. Sometimes, people nonchalantly tried to get Bernadette to touch one of their possessions. She knew what people were after and on one occasion, she told a bishop who purposely dropped his skullcap on her bed to pick it up himself!

The Eucharist bathes the tormented soul in light and love. Then the soul appreciates these words: "Come all you who are sick, I will restore your health."

St. Bernadette Soubirous
—Personal Notes

Bernadette called her sickbed the "White Chapel" because her bed was surrounded by white curtains. Bernadette suffered from ill health all of her life and ultimately died a very painful death from asthma and tuberculosis. One time, she said, "This morning after Holy Communion, I asked Our Lord for a five minute respite so I could talk comfortably with him, but he was unwilling to give it to me. My passion will last until I die."[3]

Our Lady said to Bernadette, "I do not promise to make you happy in this world, but in the next." Cardinal Francis Xavier Nguyên Van Thuân of Vietnam meditated on these words while he was in Lourdes in 1957 and said, "I had the deep impression that these words were also addressed to me. I accepted this message, though not without some fear." The Cardinal returned to Lourdes every year and continued to wonder how these words applied to him. Then "the year 1975 arrived and with it my arrest on the Feast of the Assumption, my imprisonment, my isolation. Then I understood that the Blessed Mother had been preparing me for this since 1957!"[5]

Cardinal Van Thuân was imprisoned by the Communists for thirteen years, nine of them in solitary confinement. His book, *Testimony of Hope*, is a compilation of twenty-two spiritual exercises that were presented to Pope John Paul II and the Roman Curia in 2000. He died on September 16, 2002, in Vatican City.

Bernadette never boasted, believing that the Blessed Virgin must have chosen her because she was "the most ignorant." One may think that she was canonized on December 8, 1933, because of what happened to her at Lourdes. It was actually how she lived her entire life that elevated her to ultimate glory. Pope Pius XI said, "There is no doubt that here we are in the presence of saintliness in the exact and precise sense of the word. Indeed, when we consider the life of Bernadette as it has emerged from all phases of the Process . . . it can be summed up in three words: Bernadette was faithful to her mission, she was humble in her glory, and she was strong when put to the test."[4]

Our Lady of the Waters

On the day of her death, Sr. Nathalie Portat recorded Bernadette's last words: "Holy Mary, Mother of God, pray for me, poor sinner . . . poor sinner . . . Holy Mary, Mother of God, pray for me, poor sinner . . . poor sinner."

—Some of Bernadette's Sayings

Visitors to Nevers are free to walk in the garden of the Saint-Gildard convent to see the statue, known as Our Lady of the Waters, that Bernadette thought most resembled the Blessed Virgin. On the grounds, a replica of the Grotto at Lourdes was built after her death. The Chapel of St. Joseph was her original resting place. Now the main chapel holds her incorrupt body in a beautiful glass and gold reliquary.

A visitor seeing the body of St. Bernadette for the first time is moved to silence. One author stated, "Here in some way Bernadette lives on. . . . Here Bernadette is carrying on day by day, in the presence of each pilgrim, the work which the 'Immaculate Conception' gave her in the name of God. She reminds us that God is Love and that he never stops calling on us to pass from the night of our sin to his wondrous Light."[6]

O Bernadette,
in the world's eyes,
you seemed to be a most unlikely recipient of God's grace;
yet you trusted in the Lord
and faithfully carried out the mission entrusted to you.
We too must trust in Jesus
knowing that with his help
we too can accomplish whatever he asks of us,
for nothing is impossible with God. Amen

Prayer of a Poor Beggar To Jesus
(Bernadette often said this prayer)

O Jesus, give me, I beg you,
the bread of humility,
the bread of obedience,
the bread of charity,
the bread of strength to break my will and to mold it to yours,
the bread of interior mortification,
the bread of detachment from creatures,
the patience to bear the sufferings of my poor heart.

Jesus, you want me to be crucified, *fiat.*

Give me:
the bread of strength to suffer as I ought,
the bread of seeing you alone in all things and at all times,
Jesus,
Mary,
the Cross,
I want no other friends but these.

✣ Twenty-three ✣
Thérèse of Lisieux

In 1997, Pope John Paul II proclaimed St. Thérèse of Lisieux a Doctor of the Church, someone who, like Sts. Thomas Aquinas and Augustine, made a lasting and significant contribution to the Church. It would seem remarkable that the Catholic Church would uphold the life and words of a twenty-four year old girl as a model of holiness and wisdom. Her only earthly legacy was an autobiography written at the request of her superiors. But today, her heavenly legacy reaches to every corner of the earth.

I feel that my mission is about to begin—my mission to help others love God as I love Him, to give my Little Way to souls. If God grants my wish, my Heaven will be here on earth, until the end of the world. Yes, I want to spend my Eternity doing good on earth.[1]

—St. Thérèse of Lisieux

Thérèse Martin was born in Alençon in Normandy in 1873. She was the last child of Zélie and Louis Martin who both explored entering religious life before their marriage. Our intimate knowledge of Thérèse's life comes from manuscripts she wrote at the request of her sister called *Histoire d'une Ame* or *Story of a Soul*. These writings show us her journey from beloved baby sister to sainthood.

St. Thérèse of Lisieux

Thérèse, as described by her mother Zélie in letters to her family, was very intelligent, sensitive and warm-hearted. She was raised in a family where the Mass, prayer, spiritual reading and good works were the foundation of their lives. Even as a child, Thérèse's awareness of God was far beyond her years. When her sister Céline asked her how God could be present in such a small host, Thérèse replied, "That is not surprising, God is all powerful."[2] Thérèse believed that she had never gone more than three minutes in her life without thinking about God.

When Thérèse was four-and-a-half years old, her mother died and the family moved to Lisieux to be near the Guérins, her mother's family. Thérèse became introverted, shy and very prone to tears. When her beloved sister Pauline entered the Carmel, Thérèse became gravely ill. Her father requested that a novena of Masses be said at Notre Dame des Victoires in Paris, begging Our Lady to cure his daughter. On Pentecost, May 13, 1883, with her sisters Marie, Léonie and Céline by her side, Thérèse saw the family statue of the Blessed Virgin Mary smile at her, a smile that penetrated her soul. Immediately, her sickness left her.

Thérèse's First Communion remained always engraved upon her heart. "Ah! How sweet was that first kiss of Jesus!" she writes in her autobiography, "It was a kiss of love; I felt I was loved, and I said: 'I love You, and I give myself to You forever!' There were no demands made, no struggles, no sacrifices; for a long time now Jesus and poor little Thérèse looked at and

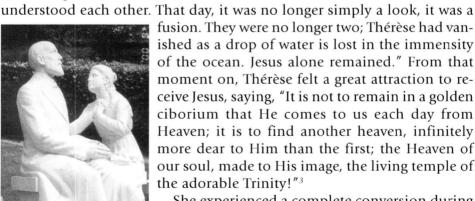

Zélie and Louis Martin were declared Venerable by Pope John Paul II in 1994. Of their daughters, four became Carmelites and one became a Visitation nun. Zélie's letters are full of happy glimpses into the Martin's home and show a mother most concerned about raising her daughters to be good Christians.

After the death of his wife, Louis' two daughters, Pauline and Marie, entered the Carmel in Lisieux. When Thérèse was fifteen, he joyfully, but not without sadness, gave his little "Queen" Thérèse to the Lord as His spouse saying that God had indeed blessed him by asking for his children. He suffered from mental illness during the last years of his life and, after his death, Céline joined her three sisters in the same Carmelite monastery. The tombs of Zélie and Louis are in the Basilica of St. Thérèse in Lisieux.

understood each other. That day, it was no longer simply a look, it was a fusion. They were no longer two; Thérèse had vanished as a drop of water is lost in the immensity of the ocean. Jesus alone remained." From that moment on, Thérèse felt a great attraction to receive Jesus, saying, "It is not to remain in a golden ciborium that He comes to us each day from Heaven; it is to find another heaven, infinitely more dear to Him than the first; the Heaven of our soul, made to His image, the living temple of the adorable Trinity!"[3]

She experienced a complete conversion during Christmas in 1886 when some words spoken by her father caused her to regain the spirit and strength she had lost after her mother died. "I experienced a great desire to work for the conver-

St. Thérèse with her Father

sion of sinners," she writes, "a desire I hadn't felt

Léonie Martin is often the forgotten sister because unlike Pauline, Marie, Céline and Thérèse, she did not become a Carmelite but entered the Visitation order, founded by St. Francis de Sales and St. Jane Frances de Chantal. Of all her children, Zélie Martin worried most about Léonie. She was rebellious, hard to control and a poor student. Léonie said that she wanted to become a true religious and a saint. Her mother said, "Unless a miracle is worked, my Léonie will never enter a religious community" and, indeed, Léonie tried to enter a religious order three times.

In 1888, Thérèse said, "We must not worry that Léonie's attempts at religious life have been unsuccessful. After my death, she will enter the Visitation Order, and this time she will succeed; she will take my name, and that of St. Francis de Sales." In 1899, Léonie became a Visitation nun and received the name Sister Françoise-Thérèse. When she died in 1941, Cardinal Suhard said that she had been "a flower of holiness whom the Lord came to pluck from the Visitation garden to unite her to that other flower."[4] The other flower is St. Thérèse who is known as the Little Flower.

so intensely before. I felt charity enter my soul, and the need to forget myself and to please others."[5]

When Thérèse was fourteen, she wanted to enter the Carmel like her two older sisters but she was told that she was too young. After appealing to the bishop, her father took her on a pilgrimage to Rome to celebrate the jubilee of Pope Leo XIII. Thérèse decided to appeal to the Holy Father himself. During a general audience, Thérèse grasped the hand of the pope and asked for permission to become a Carmelite. The pope replied that she should do what her superiors told her to do. After more pleading by Thérèse, he said to her, "You will enter if God wills it."[6]

Thérèse finally was granted permission to enter the Carmel in 1888 when she was fifteen. In religious life, she signed her name as: Marie, Françoise, Thérèse of the Child Jesus and the Holy Face. She said she had come to save souls, and especially pray for priests.

I had the unspeakable consolation of receiving Holy Communion every day. Ah! This was sweet indeed! Jesus spoiled me for a long time, much longer than He did His faithful spouses, for He permitted me to receive Him while the rest didn't have the same happiness. I was very fortunate, too, to touch the sacred vessels and to prepare the little linen cloths destined to come in contact with Jesus. I felt that I should be fervent and recalled frequently these words spoken to a holy deacon: "You are to be holy, you who carry the vessels of the Lord" (Isaiah 52:11).

—St. Thérèse of Lisieux
Story of a Soul

In 1893, Thérèse was made assistant to the novice mistress. In answer to her prayers, she corresponded with a seminarian, Maurice Bellière, who asked the Carmelites to pray for the salvation of his soul and for his vocation as a missionary priest. Maurice and Thérèse became spiritual brother and sister.

When I was starting to learn the history of France, the story of Joan of Arc's exploits delighted me. I used to feel in my heart the desire and courage to imitate her. It seemed to me that the Lord destined me too for great things. I was not mistaken. But instead of voices from Heaven calling me to combat, I heard in the depths of my soul a voice that was gentler and stronger still: the voice of the Spouse of virgins was calling me to other exploits and more glorious conquests, and in the solitude of Carmel I understood my mission was not to crown a mortal king but to make the King of Heaven loved, to conquer for Him the kingdom of hearts. [7]

—St. Thérèse to Maurice

Her vocation was love. "I understood that the Church had a Heart and that this Heart was BURNING WITH LOVE. I understood it was Love alone that made the Church members act, and if Love ever became extinct, apostles would not preach the Gospel and martyrs would not shed their blood. I understood that LOVE COMPRISED ALL VOCATIONS, THAT LOVE WAS EVERYTHING, THAT IT EMBRACED ALL TIMES AND PLACES. . . . IN A WORD, THAT IT WAS ETERNAL!" [8]

A few months before her death, Thérèse was asked to describe her "Little Way." She said, "It is the way of spiritual childhood, the way of trust and absolute surrender." [9] She lived this Little Way herself during the last months of her life. She experienced extreme spiritual desolation, feelings of abandonment and despair. Yet she clung ever tighter to Jesus in the midst of her dark journey saying she chose to believe. Her last written words in her autobiography were, "I go to Him with confidence and love . . . " [10]

Thérèse received the Sacrament of the Sick in the summer of 1897 when she had the happiness "of seeing Jesus in the Blessed Sacrament leave the tabernacle to come to me, whom I received as Viaticum for my long voyage! This Bread of Heaven has strengthened me. Just look, it seems as if my pilgrimage can't get to its destination. Far from complaining about this, I rejoice that God still lets me suffer for love of Him. Ah, how good it is to let yourself go in His arms, with neither fears nor desires." She told Maurice, "I am not dying; I am entering life." [11]

Thérèse died on October 4, 1897. Her *Histoire d'une Ame* was finished only a few months before her death and was published the following year. Thérèse was canonized in 1925 and she is the patroness of the missions along with St. Francis Xavier and Patroness of France along with Joan of Arc. Pope Pius X called her the greatest saint in modern times.

The Spirit of truth opened and made known to her what he usually hides from the wise and prudent and reveals to little ones; thus she enjoyed such knowledge of the things above . . . that she shows everyone else the sure way to salvation.[12]

—Pope Pius XI

In Lisieux today, a magnificent basilica has been built in her honor. The Carmelite chapel contains her remains and also the statue of the Virgin Mary that was in her room when she was miraculously cured. Thérèse's childhood home in Lisieux, Les Buissonnets, can be visited as well as her home in Alençon. The Cathedral of St. Pierre in Lisieux is where Thérèse attended Mass. The side chapel was built by Pierre Cauchon, the man who presided over Joan of Arc's trial.

O Thérèse,
from your family
came plentiful vocations to work in the Lord's vineyard.
We pray that all parents respond generously
to the call of the Holy Spirit
and nurture in their children a love for God
and a desire to serve Him no matter where He calls them.
O Jesus, fill us with the zeal of St. Thérèse. Amen.

Prayer to Jesus in the Tabernacle[13]
(Composed by St. Thérèse, dated July 16, 1895)

O Jesus hidden in the prison of the tabernacle!
    I come with joy to you each evening
  to thank you for the graces you have given me. . . .
O Jesus!
How happy I would be if I had been faithful, but alas,
    often in the evening I am sad
    because I feel I could have corresponded better with your graces. . . .
    If I were more united to You,
    more charitable with my sisters,
    more humble and more mortified,
    I would feel less sorrow when I talk to you in prayer.
And yet, O my God,
    very far from becoming discouraged
    at the sight of my miseries,
    I come to You with confidence
    recalling that "those who are well do not need a doctor,
    but the sick do."
I beg You then to cure me and to pardon me.
    I will keep in mind Lord,
    "that the soul to whom you have forgiven more
    should also love You more than the others. . . ."
    I offer You every beat of my heart
    as so many acts of love and reparation
    and I unite them to Your infinite merits.
I beg You, O my Divine Bridegroom,
    to be the Restorer of my soul,
    to act in me despite my resistance;
    and lastly, I wish to have no other will but Yours.
    Tomorrow, with the help of your grace,
    I will begin a new life in which each moment
    will be an act of love and renunciation.

Thus, after coming each evening to the foot of your altar,
    I will finally reach the last evening of my life.
Then will begin for me the unending day of eternity
    when I will place in Your Divine Heart
    the struggles of exile! Amen.

✤ *Twenty-four* ✤
Sacré-Coeur

A familiar sight to all who visit Paris is the basilica of Sacré-Coeur that stands watch over the city from its place high on the Hill of Martyrs or Montmartre. Adoration of the Blessed Sacrament, initiated here in 1885, has never ceased. Sacré-Coeur is a reminder to the people of France and to the world that the Lord is constantly watching over us. It is also a reminder for us to come and visit with Him.

When Pope John Paul II visited Montmartre in 1980, he said, "We come here to meet the heart pierced for us, from which water and blood gush. It is the redeeming love, which is at the origin of salvation, of our salvation, which is at the origin of the Church. . . . At every moment, we are enveloped, the whole world is enveloped, in the love of this heart 'which loved men so much and which is so little loved by them.'"[1]

During Roman times, Montmartre was known as *Mons Martis* (Hill of Mars) or *Mons Mercurii* (Hill of Mercury). Around the year 250 AD, St. Denis, the first bishop of Paris, was martyred. According to tradition, he carried his head over Montmartre to the vicinity of the Basilica of Saint-Denis where he died. Hence the name *Mons Martyrum* or Hill of Martyrs came to be associated with blood spilled for the Faith. A chapel called the *Sanctum Martyrium* was built to commemorate Denis' martyrdom. On August 15, 1534, St. Ignatius of Loyola, St. Francis Xavier and their companions met in the crypt of this chapel and formed the beginning of the Society of Jesus or Jesuits.

Basilica of Sacré-Coeur

The stories of St. Denis are considered "preposterous" today, writes James Broderick, SJ, a biographer of St. Ignatius. Says Fr. Broderick, "St. Ignatius was not troubled by our modern misgivings about the early history of the French church, no more

St. Madeleine
Sophie Barat

than was St. Thomas of Canterbury who went to pray in the little chapel on Montmartre a year before his own martyrdom. By such happenings, but above all from the devotion of St. Ignatius of Loyola, the place acquired a heavenly authenticity in the absence of an earthly one."

—Saint Ignatius Of Loyola:
The Pilgrim Years 1491–1538

In 1147, a Benedictine abbey was consecrated on Montmartre by St. Bernard and Pope Eugenius III. The Abbey Church, Saint-Pierre du Montmartre, is one of the oldest surviving churches in Paris. The last abbess was executed in 1794 during the Revolution and the convent was razed. For the next one hundred years, Montmartre became known more for the Bohemian lifestyle of the writers, artists and musicians who inhabited the area.

In 1871, the Prussians took Paris during the Franco-Prussian War and the people of France vowed to build a church dedicated to the Sacred Heart if they were delivered from their misery. Cardinal Guillot, archbishop of Paris, decided on Montmartre as the site of a basilica saying, "It is here that the Sacred Heart should be enthroned, to draw all to itself, on the summit of the hill upon which Christendom was born in the blood of the first apostles, here that the

One of the most notable orders named in honor of the Sacred Heart is the Society of the Sacred Heart whose first superior was St. Madeleine Sophie Barat. She was born in Joigny in Burgundy in 1779. Her brother Louis, later a Jesuit priest, ensured that she had a thorough education. It was Louis who introduced her to a priest who was seeking women to join a new congregation devoted to the education of young women. At age twenty-three, she was elected superior and despite her reservations, she surrendered to what she viewed as the will of God. The first school was started in Amiens and by the time of her death, there were over eighty houses around the world.

Describing Holy Communion, she said, "Our Lord knew well that we were too weak to walk courageously along the road of life that is often very difficult. So His prophet who saw from afar all the treasures hidden in the Church of Jesus Christ said, 'Thou hast prepared a table before me, against them that afflict me' (Psalm 23:5). The food of this table is Jesus Christ Himself; His Divine Flesh, His precious Blood. It is He who prepares the feast and invites us to it."[2]

Mother Barat died in Paris in 1865 and was canonized in 1925. In 1904, because of the expulsion of religious orders from France, her body was taken to Jette, Belgium, where it remains today. One of her most famous daughters was St. Rose Philippine Duchesne, a missionary to America, who died in St. Charles, Missouri, in 1852.

Venerable Charles de Foucauld was born in Strasbourg, France, in 1858, into a very wealthy family. Calling himself selfish, irreligious and utterly wicked, he was a scandal to his family. He confided to a priest that he had trouble believing in God. He was told, "What is missing now, in order for you to believe, is a pure heart. Go down on your knees, make your confession to God, and you will believe." He did so and after receiving Communion, he left the church feeling "that infinite peace, that dazzling light, that unfailing happiness." He said, "As soon as I came to believe there was a God, I understood that I could not do otherwise than to live only for him."

He entered religious life and eventually went to Algeria to live among the Moslems in extreme solitude in the Sahara Desert. Brother Michael, his companion for awhile, said, "He loved Jesus Christ passionately, and his great happiness was in conversing with the prisoner of love, really present in the tabernacle. Prayer was his delight. It was truly his life and the breath of his soul. He spent the greater part of his days and nights kneeling before the Blessed Sacrament, adoring, pleading, thanking, atoning. To the end of my life I shall remember the Mass of Father Charles, which I had the great fortune to serve."[3]

Charles was murdered in 1916 in Tamanrasset, Algeria. Though his companions in the desert were few, his witness led others to follow his example after his death. His cause for canonization is underway.

Ven. Charles de Foucauld

monument to our religious rebirth should be raised."[4]

The architect, Paul Abadie, erected a Byzantine-style basilica that was consecrated in 1919. The money for the church was donated by the people of France, including St. Thérèse who gave a gold bracelet. This was abhorrent to those who wanted to eradicate religion from France and who considered the basilica to be "the outrage of the nineteenth century." Montmartre again became a sacred place. "Its graceful silhouette and 'bouquet of chapels' stand out lofty and incorruptible from the crowded plain as the image of a spiritual power brooding over Paris."[5]

We are at Montmartre, in the Basilica of the Sacred Heart, consecrated to the contemplation of Christ's love present in the Blessed Sacrament. We are called not only to meditate on, and contemplate, this mystery of Christ's love; we are called to take part in it. It is the mystery of the Holy Eucharist, the center of our faith, the center of our worship of Christ's merciful love manifested in His Sacred heart, a mystery adored here day and night, in this basilica, which thereby becomes one of those centers from which the Lord's love and grace radiate in a mysterious but real way on your city, on your country, and on the redeemed world.[6]

—Pope John Paul II

At the entrance to the Basilica, a statue of the Sacred Heart of Jesus stands above two equestrian statues of Joan of Arc and St. Louis. The four stained glass windows in the narthex honor St. Margaret Mary, St. John Eudes, St. Gertrude (a German mystic who had visions of the Sacred Heart) and Charles de Foucauld, a pilgrim to Montmartre.

Inside the basilica is a monumental mosaic of Jesus exposing His heart of gold, flanked by His mother and St. Michael. Surrounding Him are the people in history who have honored His Sacred Heart. The Latin inscription underneath reads: "To the most holy Heart of Jesus, France, fervent, penitent and grateful." In the crypt is a plaque commemorating the visit of St. Thérèse of Lisieux who came as a pilgrim with her father and sister and consecrated herself to the Sacred Heart. The great bell tower houses the famous Savoyarde bell, one of the largest in the world.

Eucharistic adoration has continued day and night at Sacré-Coeur for over one hundred years. Even when the Nazis controlled Paris and bombs destroyed some of the stained glass windows, adoration did not cease. Here, as Pope John Paul II said, "Christians gather in succession to seek 'the unsearchable riches of Christ'" (Eph 3:8).[7] The Lord asked St. Margaret Mary to spend one hour a week with Him in prayer. At Sacré-Coeur, the faithful ensure that someone remains with Jesus every hour of every day. By these prayers, France, the world, and all of us can bring about the conversion of all hearts.

O Jesus,
what is needed for peace and love to reign in the world,
is devotion to your Sacred Heart.
It starts with me;
help me to love more, give more, pray more.
Like Charles de Foucauld,
help me to abandon my selfish desires
and instead live for others. Amen.

Consecration of the Human Race to the Sacred Heart of Jesus

(Issued by His Holiness, Pope Pius XI, December 11, 1925)

Most sweet Jesus, Redeemer of the human race,
Look down upon us humbly prostrate before You.
  We are Yours and Yours we wish to be.
But to be more surely united with You,
  Behold each one of us freely consecrates ourselves today,
  To Your Most Sacred Heart.

Many indeed have never known You,
  Many, too, despising Your precepts, have rejected You.
Have mercy on them all, most merciful Jesus,
  And draw them to Your Sacred Heart.
Be Thou King, O Lord,
  Not only of the faithful who have never forsaken You,
  But also of the prodigal children who have abandoned You.
Grant that they may quickly return to their Father's house,
  Lest they die of wretchedness and hunger.

Be Thou King of those who are deceived by erroneous opinions,
  Or whom discord keeps aloof,
  And call them back to the harbor of truth and unity of faith,
  So that soon there may be
  But one flock and one Shepherd.

Grant, O Lord, to Your Church,
  Assurance of freedom and immunity from harm;
  Give peace and order to all nations,
  And make the earth resound from pole to pole with one cry;
  Praise to the Divine Heart that wrought our salvation;
  to It be glory and honor forever. Amen.

Endnotes

The Fleur-de-Lys

1. Gregory of Tours, *History of the Franks*, in *Readings in Church History*, ed. Coleman J. Barry, OSB (Westminster, MD: The Newman Press, 1962), 214, 215.

1. Mary Magdalene

1. Louis de Montfort, *Love of Eternal Wisdom* in *God Alone* (Bay Shore, NY: Montfort Publications, 1999), 84.
2. Luigi Borriello, OCD, *Spiritual Doctrine of Blessed Elizabeth of the Trinity*, trans. Jordan Aumann, OP (Staten Island: Alba House, 1986) 34. Blessed Elizabeth of the Trinity was a Carmelite from Dijon who died at age 26. She was beatified by Pope John Paul II in 1984.
3. Pope John Paul II, *France: Message of Peace, Trust, Love and Faith*, comp. Daughters of St. Paul (Boston: Pauline Editions, 1980), 110.
4. *Butler's Lives of Patron Saints*, ed. Michael Walsh (San Francisco: Harper and Row, 1987), 53.
5. Elisabeth Leseur, *My Spirit Rejoices* (Manchester, NH: Sophia Institute Press, 1996), 240. From Elisabeth's journal, discovered after her death by her husband Felix in 1914. As she predicted, Felix, who had lost his faith, entered religious life and was ordained a priest. Her cause for canonization has been opened.
6. Ibid., 163.

2. Notre-Dame de Fourvière

1. H. M. Gillett, *Famous Shrines of Our Lady* (Westminster, MD: The Newman Press, 1952), 118.
2. Irenaeus, *Against Heresies* in *The Faith of the Early Fathers*, vol.1, ed. William A. Jurgens (Collegeville, Minn: The Liturgical Press, 1970), 90, 95.

3. Dom Antoine Marie, "Newsletter on Pauline Jaricot to Friends of Saint Joseph Abbey," issued from Abbaye Saint-Joseph Clairval in Flavigny-sur-Ozerain, France (June 22, 2001).
4. Gillett, *Shrines*, 120.
5. André Guitton, *Peter Julian Eymard: Apostle of the Eucharist*, trans. Conrad Goulet (Ponteranica, Italy: Centro Eucharistico, 1996), 73.
6. Pope John Paul II, "Seek the Good of the Citizens, Especially the Marginalized," *L'Osservatore Romano*, October 13, 1986.

3. Mont Saint-Michel

1. Henry Adams, *Mont Saint-Michel and Chartres* (New York: The Heritage Press, 1957), 1.
2. Lucien Bély, *Mont Saint-Michel*, trans. Paul Williams and Angela Moyon (Rennes, France: Editions Ouest-France: 1992), 15-16.
3. *'Neath St. Michael's Shield* (Boston: Pauline Books & Media, 1977), 3.
4. Michel Carrouges, *Père Jacques*, trans. Salvator Attanasio (New York: The MacMillan Co., 1961), 254.
5. Francis J. Murphy, *Père Jacques: Resplendent in Victory* (Washington: ICS Publications, 1998), 168.
6. Adams, *Mont Saint-Michel*, 40.

4. Bernard of Clairvaux

1. Theodore Ratisbonne, *St. Bernard of Clairvaux* (Rockford, Ill: TAN Books and Publishers, Inc., 1991), 2, 5.
2. George Shuster, *The Worlds Great Catholic Literature*. (Gardern City, NY: Halycon House, 1942), 297.
3. H.C. Graef, *The Way of the Mystics* (Cork: The Mercier Press, 1948), 11.

129

4. Bruno Scott James, *St. Bernard of Clairvaux* (London: Hodder and Stoughton, 1957), 23.
5. Leon Cristiani, *St. Bernard of Clairvaux* (Boston: Daughters of St. Paul, 1983), 24.
6. Bruno Scott James, *St. Bernard of Clairvaux: Seen Through His Selected Letters* (Chicago: Henry Regnery, 1953), 170.
7. James, *Letters*, vii.
8. James Snyder, *Medieval Art* (New York: Harry N. Abrams, 1989), 274.
9. Cristiani, *St. Bernard*, 74.
10. James, St. Bernard, 117.
11. Ratisbonne, *St. Bernard*, 256.
12. Shuster, *Great Catholic Literature*, 37.
13. E. I. Watkin, *Neglected Saints* (San Francisco: Ignatius Press, 1955), 225.
14. Ratisbonne, *St. Bernard*, xiii.
15. Graef, *Mystics*, 20.
16. Ibid., 15.
17. Ibid., 17.
18. Cristiani, *St. Bernard*, 170.
19. John Hardon, *Treasury of Catholic Wisdom* (San Francisco: Ignatus Press, 1987), 191.

5. Notre-Dame
1. Hilaire Belloc, *Paris* (London: Methuen, 1929), 8.
2. *Notre-Dame* (Paris: Connaissance des Arts, 1997), 70.
3. Ibid., 4.
4. Daniel Sargent, *Four Independents* (New York: Sheed and Ward, 1935), 82.

6. King Louis IX
1. John of Joinville, *The Character of St. Louis,* trans. René Hague (Lawrence, KS: Coronado Press, 1968), 7.
2. Margaret Wade Labarge, *Saint Louis* (Boston: Little, Brown & Co., 1968), 21.
3. *Saint Louis: King of France* (London: Sands & Co., 1913), 173.
4. René de La Croix Castries, *The Lives of the Kings and Queens of France*, trans.

Anne Dobell (New York: Albert A. Knopf, 1979), 75.
5. Joinville, *The Character of St. Louis*, 36.
6. Alan Temko, *Notre-Dame of Paris*, (New York: The Viking Press, 1955), 270.
7. *Saint Louis: King of France*, 182.
8. Stefano M. Manelli, FFI, *Jesus, Our Eucharistic Love* (New Bedford, MA: Franciscan Friars of the Immaculate, 1996), 15, 20.
9. Louis Grodecki, *Sainte-Chapelle* (Paris: Caisse Nationale Des Monuments Historiques), 5.
10. Cardinal Francis George, OMI, "Making Faith Visible: French Catholic Thought and World Youth Day, Paris, 1997", *Lumen Christi*, Vol.1 No. 2 (Spring 2002): 9.
11. *Saint Louis: King of France*, 252.
12. Labarge, *Saint Louis*, 163.
13. Ibid., 216.
14. John of Joinville, *The Life of St. Louis,* trans. and ed. René Hague (New York: Sheed and Ward, 1955), 25.

7. Chartres
1. Malcolm Miller, *Chartres Cathedral* (United Kingdom: Pitkin Unichrome, 1996), 9.
2. Hilary of Poitiers, *The Trinity* in *The Fathers of the Church*, trans. Stephen McKenna, CSSR (New York: Fathers of the Church, 1954), 286.
3. Warren H. Carroll, *The Building of Christendom*, Vol. 2 of *A History of Christendom* (Front Royal, VA: Christendom College Press, 1987), 280.
4. Watkin, *Neglected Saints*, 16.
5. Christopher Donaldson, *Martin of Tours* (London: Routledge & Kegan, 1980), 153.
6. Daniel Halévy, *Peguy* (New York, NY: Longmans, Green and Co., 1947), 217.
7. Carroll, *Building of Christendom*, 265.
8. Miller, *Chartres*, 93.

8. Joan of Arc

1. Leon Cristiani, *St. Joan of Arc* (Boston: St. Paul Books & Media, 1977), 28.
2. Ibid., 36.
3. Regine Pernoud and Marie-Véronique Clin, *Joan of Arc: Her Story*, trans. Jeremy duQuesnay (New York: St. Martin's Press, 1999), 23, 30.
4. Francis Talbot, SJ, *Saint Among the Savages: The Life of Isaac Jogues* (New York: Harper and Brothers, 1935), 337, 399.
5. Carl Koch, *Praying with John Baptist de la Salle* (Winona, Minn: Saint Mary's Press, Christian Brothers Publications, 1990), 48.
6. Pernoud, *Joan of Arc: Her Story*, 154.
7. *The Trial of Joan of Arc*, a verbatim report of the proceedings from the Orleans Manuscript, trans. W. S. Scott (London: The Folio Society, 1968), 161.
8. Pernoud, *Joan of Arc: Her Story*, 136.
9. Cristiani, *St. Joan of Arc*, 148.
10. Pernoud, *Joan of Arc: Her Story*, 137.

9. Francis de Sales

1. André Ravier, SJ, *Francis de Sales: Sage and Saint* (San Francisco: Ignatius Press, 1988), 23.
2. Ibid., 32, 38.
3. Ibid., 56.
4. Ibid., 59.
5. Ibid., 67.
6. Michael de la Bedoyere, *Saint Maker: The Remarkable Life of St. Francis de Sales* (Manchester NH: Sophia Institute Press, 1998), 93.
7. Ibid., xiii.
8. Ibid., 113, 125.
9. Ibid., 231.
10. Arthur R. McGratty, SJ, *The Sacred Heart: Yesterday and Today* (New York: Benziger Brothers, 1951), 57.
11. Bedoyere, *Saint Maker*, 281.

10. Vincent de Paul

1. Mary Purcell, *The World of Monsieur Vincent* (Chicago: Loyola University Press, 1989), 35.
2. F. A. Forbes, *Saint Vincent de Paul* (Rockford: TAN Books and Publishers, 1998), 17.
3. Purcell, *Monsieur Vincent*, 73.
4. J.B. Boudignon, *St. Vincent de Paul*, trans. Patrick Finney, CM (St. Louis: The Vincentian Press, 1925), 399. Father Etienne was the former superior of the Vincentians and Daughters of Charity.
5. Kathryn B. La Fleur, SP, *St. Louise de Marillac: A Light in the Darkness* (Hyde Park, NY: New City Press, 1996), 96, 115.
6. Purcell, *Monsieur Vincent*, 82.
7. Forbes, *St. Vincent*, 48.
8. Purcell, *Monsieur Vincent*, 165.
9. La Fleur, *St. Louise*, 96.

11. John Francis Regis

1. Albert S. Foley, SJ, *St. Regis: Social Crusader* (Milwaukee: The Bruce Publishing Co., 1941), 13.
2. Ibid., 75.
3. M. Assumpta O'Hanlon, OP, *St. Dominic, Servant But Friend* (St. Louis: B. Herder Book Co., 1954), 61.
4. Foley, *St. Regis*, 154, 155.
5. Ibid., 100, 195.
6. Robert E. Holland, SJ, *Life of St. John Francis Regis* (Chicago: Loyola University Press, 1922), 88.
7. Rawley Myers, *The Saints Show us Christ: Daily Readings on the Spiritual Life* (San Francisco: Ignatius Press, 1996), 35.
8. Foley, *St. Regis*, 222.
9. *At Prayer With Saint Thérèse Couderc*, ed. Rose F. Hoover, RC (Chicago: Religious of the Cenacle, 1999), 29.

12. Margaret Mary Alacoque

1. Graef, *Mystics*, 110.
2. Leon Cristiani, *St. Margaret Mary and the Promises of the Sacred Heart* (Bos-

ton: Daughters of St. Paul, 1984), 135.
3. Ibid., 22.
4. Margaret Mary Alacoque, *The Autobiography of St. Margaret Mary*, trans. Vincent Kerns (Westminister, MD: The Newman Press, 1961), 19.
5. Cristiani, *St. Margaret Mary*, 50.
6. Margaret Yeo, *These Three Hearts* (Milwaukee: The Bruce Publishing Co., 1940), 205.
7. Cristiani, *St. Margaret Mary*, 83.
8. Margaret Mary, *Autobiography*, 44.
9. Timothy T. O'Donnell, *Heart of the Redeemer* (San Francisco: Ignatius Press, 1992), 131.
10. Claude de la Colombière, *The Spiritual Direction of St. Claude de la Colombière*, trans. Mother M. Philip, IBVM (San Francisco: Ignatius Press, 1998), 9.
11. Yeo, *These Three Hearts*, 210.
12. Ibid., x.
13. O'Donnell, *Heart*, 135.
14. Graef, *Mystics*, 111.

13. Louis de Montfort

1. John Paul II, "Martyrs in the Vendée Courageously Remained Faithful to Christ's Church," *L'Osservatore Romano*, September 25, 1996.
2. Eddie Doherty, *Wisdom's Fool* (Bay Shore, NY: Montfort Publications, 1993), 34.
3. Montfort, *True Devotion to Mary in God Alone*, 335.
4 Doherty, *Wisdom's Fool*, 62.
5. Montfort, *Love of Eternal Wisdom in God Alone*, 52.
6. John Paul II, "Vendée," *L'Osservatore Romano*.
7. Benedetta Papasogli, *Wisdom of the Heart: The Story of Marie Louise Trichet* (Bay Shore, NY: Montfort Publications, 1993), 28, 271.
8. Doherty, *Wisdom's Fool*, 105.
9. Ibid., 113, 100.
10. Ibid., 137.

14. The Martyrs of Compiègne

1. Warren H. Carroll, *The Guillotine and the Cross* (Front Royal, VA: Christendom Press, 1991), 177.
2. *St. Julie Billiart: A Saint For Our Time*, adapted from *Rose of Picardy* by Sr. Anna of the Sacred Heart McCarthy, SNDdeN (Cincinnati: Sisters of Notre Dame de Namur, 2000), 14.
3. William Bush, *To Counter the Terror* (Washington, DC: ICS Publications, 1999), 188.
4. Ibid., 48.
5. Ibid., 209.
6. Borriello, *Elizabeth*, 46.
7. *Catechism of the Catholic Church*, 260 (Ligouri, MO: Liguori Publications, 1994), 69. Blessed Elizabeth of the Trinity is known for her mystical writings on the Trinity and for the remarkable, holy way she approached her death.

15. John Vianney

1. Bartholomew J. O'Brien, *The Curé of Ars: Patron Saint of Parish Priests* (Rockford, IL: TAN Books and Publishers, 1987), vi.
2. George William Rutler, *The Curé D'Ars Today: St. John Vianney* (San Francisco: Ignatius Press, 1988), 252.
3. O'Brien, *The Curé of Ars*, 4.
4. John XXIII, *Sacerdotii Nostrii Primordia: Encyclical Letter of His Holiness Pope John XXIII On The Priesthood*, (Washington, DC: National Catholic Welfare Conference, 1959), 18.
5. Francis Trochu, *Curé D'Ars: A Biography of St. Jean-Marie Vianney*, trans. Ronald Matthews (Manila: Sinag-Tala Publishers, 1998), 36.
6. O'Brien, *The Curé of Ars*, 26, 30, 31.
7. Rutler, *The Curé of Ars*, 101.
8. Abbé H. Convert, *Eucharistic Meditations: Extracts from the Writings of Saint John Vianney*, trans. Mary Benvenuta, OP (Trabuco Canyon, CA: Source Books

& Anthony Clarke, 1998), 30.

9. Rutler, 257.
10. Ibid., 184, 185.
11. Convert, *Eucharistic Meditations*, 110.
12. O'Brien, 54.
13. Ibid., 83.
14. Trochu, 213.
15. John XXIII, The Priesthood, 25.

16. Jeanne Jugan

1. Gabriel-Marie Cardinal Garrone, *Poor in Spirit: The Spirituality of Jeanne Jugan*, trans. Alan Neame (London: Darton, Longman and Todd, 1975), 12.
2. Paul Milcent, *Jeanne Jugan: Humble So As To Love More*, trans. Alan Neame (London: Darton, Longman and Todd, 1981), 15.
3. Charles LeBrun, CJM, *The Spirtual Teaching of St. John Eudes*, trans. Dom Basil Whelan, OSB (London: Sands and Co., 1934), 74 .
4. Milcent, *Jeanne Jugan*, 54, 56, 70.
5. Garrone, *Poor in Spirit*, 27.
6. Milcent, *Jeanne Jugan*, 75.
7. Garrone, *Poor in Spirit*, 75, 26.
8. Ibid., 58.
9. Milcent, *Jeanne Jugan*, 208.
10. Garrone, *Poor in Spirit*, 64.
11. Milcent, *Jeanne Jugan*, 71.

17. Catherine Labouré

1. Omer Englebert, *Catherine Labouré and the Modern Apparitions of Our Lady*, trans. Alastair Guinan (New York: P. J. Kenedy and Sons, 1959), 7.
2. Joseph I. Dirvan, CM, *St. Catherine Labouré of the Miraculous Medal* (Rockford, IL: TAN Books and Publishers, 1984), 36.
3. Englebert, *Catherine Labouré*, 14.
4. Dirvan, *St. Catherine*, 74.
5. Robin Ruggles, *Apparition Shrines: Places of Pilgrimage and Prayer* (Boston: Pauline Books & Media, 2000), 87.
6. Don Sharkey, *The Woman Shall Con-*

quer (Libertyville, IL: Prow Books/ Franciscan Marytown Press, 1976), 67.
7. Bro. Francis Mary Kalvelage, FFI, ed., *Marian Shrines of France* (New Bedford, MA: Franciscan Friars of the Immaculate, 1998), 16, 17.
8. John Paul II, "Mary's Mediation Derives from Christ's," *L'Osservatore Romano*, October 8, 1977.
9. Ruggles, 39.
10. Kalvelage, *Shrines*, 42. St. Maximilian Kolbe celebrated his first Mass at San' Andrea delle Fratte where Alphonse Ratisbonne had his conversion.
11. Dirvan, *St. Catherine*, 229.

18. Peter Julian Eymard

1. Martin Dempsey, *Champion of the Blessed Sacrament* (New York: Eymard League), 5.
2. Ibid., Introduction.
3. Ibid.,14.
4. Norman B. Pelletier, SSS, *Tomorrow Will Be Too Late* (Cleveland: Emmanual Publishing, 1992), 58.
5. André Guitton, SSS, *Peter Julian Eymard: Apostle of the Eucharist* (Paris: Mediaspaul, 1992), 66.
6. Pelletier, *Tomorrow*, 71.
7. Guitton, *Peter Julian*, 199, 140.
8. Peter Julian Eymard, *How To Get More Out of Holy Communion* (Manchester, NH: Sophia Institute Press, 2000), 176.
9. Guitton, Peter Julian, 273.
10. Dempsey, *Champion*, 251.
11. Ibid., 92.
12. Peter Julian Eymard, *Communion*, 11.
13. Guitton, *Peter Julian*, 351.

19. Notre Dame des Victoires

1. Gillett, *Famous Shrines*, 171.
2. Bishop Fabian Bruskewitz, *A Bishop Speaks* (San Francisco: Ignatius Press, 1997), 414.
3. Dempsey, *Champion*, 57.
4. Marie Carmelle, ND de SION, *Theodore*

Ratisbonne: *Journey By The Light of the World*, trans. Brenda St. Lawrence, ND de SION (Rome: Gregorian Universtity, 1986), 21, 43.

5. Abbé Charles Sylvain, *Life of Reverend Father Hermann*, trans. Mrs. F. Raymond Barker (New York: P. J. Kenedy & Sons, 1925), 245.
6. Kalvelage, *Marian Shrines of France*, 195.
7. A. Auffray, SC, *Blessed Don Bosco*, an English edition by W. H. Mitchell, MA (New York: Benziger Brothers, 1930), 357.
8. Sylvain, *Father Hermann*, 247.

20. Our Lady of La Salette

1. *The Sixteen Documents of Vatican II and the Instruction on the Liturgy* (Boston: St. Paul Editions), 173.
2. *La Salette, The Apparition and the Message*, design and photos by Roger Castel (United States La Salette Congregation, 1994), 8.
3. Kalvelage, *Marian Shrines*, 49, 50.
4. Mary Alice Dennis, *Mélanie* (Rockford, IL: TAN Books and Publishing, 1995), 82, 97.
5. Roger Castel, *La Salette* (Strausbourg, France: Editions du Signe, 1995), 6.
6. Kalvelage, *Shrines*, 67.
7. Castel, *La Salette*, 42.
8. Kalvelage, *Marian Shrines*, 63.
9. Ibid., 86.
10. Jean Jaouen, MS, *A Grace Called La Salette*, trans. Normand Theroux, MS (Attleboro, MA: La Salette Publications, 1991), 296.
11. Castel, *La Salette*, 19. Maximin is buried in Corps but his heart is interred in the La Salette Basilica. Melanie died and is buried in Altamura, Italy.
12. Castel, *La Salette*, 19.

21. Our Lady of Lourdes

1. Frances Parkinson Keyes, *Bernadette of Lourdes* (Wheathampstead, England: Anthony Clarke, 1988), 92.
2. René Laurentin, *Bernadette Speaks* (Boston: Pauline Books & Media, 2000), 116.
3. Ibid., 34.
4. *The Immaculate: Special Issue on Lourdes*, "I Met a Miracle" (February, 1970).
5. André Ravier, SJ, *Bernadette: The Saint of Poverty and Light* (Nouvelle Librairie de France, 1974), 32.
6. Laurentin, 461.
7. Kalvelage, *Shrines*, 161.

22. Bernadette Soubirous

1. Laurentin, *Bernadette*, 562.
2. *Some of Bernadette's Sayings* (Nevers, France: Saint-Gildard Convent), 118.
3. Laurentin, *Bernadette Speaks*, 524.
4. Keyes, *Bernadette of Lourdes*, 139.
5. Archbishop Francis Xavier Nguyen Van Thuan, *Testimony of Hope* (Boston: Pauline Books & Media, 2000), 195.
6. André Ravier, SJ, *The Body of St. Bernadette* (Baume-les-Dames, France: Imprime par I.M.E., 1999), 15.

23. Thérèse of Lisieux

1. Marie Baudouin-Croix, *Léonie: A Difficult Life* (Dublin: Veritas Publications, 1993), 71.
2. Thérèse of Lisieux, *Story of a Soul*, trans. John Clarke, OCD (Washington, DC: ICS Publications, 1976), 27.
3. Thérèse of Lisieux, *Story of a Soul*, 77, 104.
4. Baudouin-Croix, *Léonie*, 25, 73, 117.
5. Thérèse, *Story of a Soul*, 99.
6. Ibid., 135.
7. Patrick Ahern, *Maurice and Thérèse: The Story of Love* (New York: Doubleday, 1998), 106.
8. Ibid., 194.
9. Ibid., vii.
10. Ibid., 259.
11. Ahern, *Maurice*, 209, 130.
12. Pope John Paul II, *Divini Amoris Scientia*,

October 19, 1997, from the website "catolicos.org."

13. Thérèse of Lisieux, *The Prayers of Saint Thérèse of Lisieux*, trans. Aletheia Kane, OCD (Washington: ICS Publications, 1997), 75-76.

24. Sacré-Coeur

1. Pope John Paul II, *France*, 177.
2. A. M. Barry, RSCJ, *Saint Madeleine Sophie Barat: Foundress of the Society of the Sacred Heart* (Newton, MA: Newton College of the Sacred Heart, 1959), 36.
3. Jean-Jacques Antier, *Charles de Foucauld* (San Francisco: Ignatius Press, 1999), 100, 102, 104, 252.
4. Philippe Julian, *Montmartre*, trans. Anne Carter (Oxford: Phaedon Press, 1977), 51.
5. Arthur R. McGratty, *The Sacred Heart: Yesterday and Today* (New York: Benziger Brothers, 1951), 209, 210.
6. O'Donnell, *Heart*, 231-232.
7. Pope John Paul II, *France*, 176.

Bibliography

Adams, Henry. *Mont Saint-Michel and Chartres*. New York: The Heritage Press, 1957.

Ahern, Patrick. *Maurice and Thérèse: The Story of Love*. New York: Doubleday, 1998.

Alacoque Margaret Mary. *The Autobiography of St. Margaret Mary*. Translated by Vincent Kerns. Westminster, Md: The Newman Press, 1961.

Anderson, Robert Gordon. *The Biography of a Cathedral*. New York: Longmans, Green and Co., 1944.

Antier, Jean-Jacques. *Charles de Foucauld*. San Francisco: Ignatius Press, 1999.

Antoine Marie, Dom. "Newsletter on Pauline Jaricot to Friends of St. Joseph Abbey". Flavigny-sur-Ozerain, France (June 22, 2001).

_____. "Newsletter on Hermann Cohen". (August 28, 2001).

At Prayer With Saint Thérèse Couderc. Edited by Rose F. Hoover. Chicago: Religious of the Cenacle, 1999.

Auffray, A., sc. *Blessed Don Bosco*. An English edition by W.H. Mitchell. New York: Benziger Brothers, 1930.

Barry, A..M. rscj. *Saint Madeleine Sophie Barat: Foundress of the Society of the Sacred Heart*. Newton, Ma: Newton College of the Sacred Heart, 1959.

Bedoyere, Michael de la. *Saint Maker: The Remarkable Life of St. Francis de Sales*. Manchester, NH: Sophia Institute Press, 1998.

Bély, Lucian. *Wonderful Mont Saint-Michel*. Translated by Paul Williams and Angela Moyon. Rennes, France: Editions Ouest-France, 1992.

Belloc, Hilaire. *Paris*. London: Methuen & Co., 1929.

Baudouin-Croix, Marie. *Léonie, A Difficult Life*. Dublin: Veritas Publications, 1993.

Borriello, Luigi, ocd. *Spiritual Doctrine of Blessed Elizabeth of the Trinity*. Translated by Jordan Aumann, op. Staten Island: Alba House, 1986.

Boudignon, J.B. *St. Vincent de Paul*. Translated by Patrick A. Finney, cm. St. Louis: The Vincentian Press, 1925.

Bougaud, Bishop of Laval. *History of St. Vincent de Paul*. Translated by Joseph Brady, cm. London: Longmans, Green and Co., 1899.

Broderick, James, sj. *Saint Ignatius of Loyola: The Pilgrim Years 1491-1538*. San Francisco: Ignatius Press, 1998.

Bruskewitz, Bishop Fabian. *A Bishop Speaks*. San Francisco: Ignatius Press, 1997.

Bush, William. *To Counter the Terror*. Washington: ICS Publications, 1999.

Butler's Lives of Patron Saints. Edited by Michael Walsh. San Francisco: Harper and Row, 1987.

Carmelle, Marie, ND DE SION, *Theodore Ratisbonne: Journey By the Light of the World.* Translated by Brenda St. Lawrence ND DE SION. Rome: Gregorian University, 1986.

Carroll, Warren H. *The Building of Christendom,* Vol. 2 of *A History of Christendom.* Front Royal, Va: Christendom College Press, 1987.

_____. *The Glory of Christendom,* Vol. 3 of *A History of Christendom.* Front Royal, Va: Christendom Press, 1993.

_____. *The Guillotine and the Cross.* Front Royal, Va: Christendom Press, 1991.

Carrouges, Michel. *Père Jacques.* Translated by Salvator Attanasio. New York: The MacMillan Company, 1961.

Castel, Roger. *La Salette: The Apparition and the Message.* United States La Salette Congregation, 1994.

_____. *La Salette.* Strasbourg, France: Editions du Signe, 1995.

Castries, René de La Croix. *The Lives of the Kings and Queens of France.* Translated by Anne Dobell. New York: Alfred A. Knopf, 1979.

Catechism of the Catholic Church. Ligouri, MO: Liguori Publications, 1994.

Colombière, Claude de la. *The Spiritual Direction of Saint Claude de la Colombière.* Translated by Mother M. Philip, IBVM. San Francisco: Ignatius Press, 1998.

Convert, Abbé H. *Eucharistic Meditations: Extracts From the Writings of Saint John Vianney.* Translated by Mary Benvenuta, OP. Trabuco Canyon, Ca: Source Books & Anthony Clarke, 1998.

Cristiani, Leon. *St. Bernard of Clairvaux.* Boston: Daughters of St. Paul, 1983.

_____. *St. Joan of Arc.* Boston: St. Paul Books & Media, 1977.

_____. *St. Margaret Mary and the Promises of the Sacred Heart.* Boston: Daughters of St. Paul, 1984.

Dansette, Adrien. *Religious History of Modern France,* Vol. 1. Edinburgh-London: Nelson, 1961.

Dargaud, Joseph. *The Eucharist in the Life of St. Margaret Mary.* Translated by Richard Arnandez, FSC. Kenosha, Wis: Prow Books/Franciscan Marytown Press, 1979.

Davies, Michael. *For Altar and Throne: The Rising in the Vendée.* St. Paul: The Remnant Press, 1997.

Davis, John F. *An Audience With Jesus.* Boston: St. Paul Editions, 1982.

Dempsey, Martin. *Champion of the Blessed Sacrament.* New York: Eymard League.

Dennis, Mary Alice. *Melanie.* Rockford, Ill: TAN Books & Publishing, Inc., 1995.

Dirvan, Joseph I., CM. *St. Catherine Labouré of the Miraculous Medal*. Rockford, Ill: TAN Books and Publishers Inc., 1984.

Dodin, Andre, CM. *Vincent de Paul & Charity*, Translated by Jean Marie Smith and Dennis Saunders. Hyde Park, NY: New City Press, 1993.

Doherty, Eddie. *Wisdom's Fool*. Bay Shore, NY: Montfort Publications, 1993.

Donaldson, Christopher. *Martin of Tours*. London: Routledge & Kegan Paul, Ltd., 1980.

Englebert, Omer. *Catherine Labouré and the Modern Apparitions of Our Lady*. Translated by Alastair Guinan. New York: P.J. Kenedy and Sons, 1959.

Eusebius. *The History of the Church From Christ to Constantine*. Translated by G. A. Williamson. Revised and edited by Andrew Louth. London: Penguin Books, 1989.

Eymard, Peter Julian. *How To Get More Out Of Holy Communion*. Manchester, NH: Sophia Institute Press, 2000.

Favier, Jean. *The World of Chartres*. New York: Harry N. Abrams, 1990.

Foley, Albert S, SJ. *St. Regis: Social Crusader*. Milwaukee, Wis: The Bruce Publishing Company, 1941.

Forbes, F.A. *St. Vincent de Paul*. Rockford, Ill: TAN Books and Publishers, Inc., 1998.

Garrone, Cardinal Gabriel-Marie. *Poor in Spirit: The Spirituality of Jeanne Jugan*. Translated by Alan Neame. London: Darton, Longman and Todd, 1975.

George, Cardinal Francis. "Making Faith Visible: French Catholic Thought and World Youth Day, Paris, 1997." *Lumen Christi* (Spring 2002).

Gillett, H. M. *Famous Shrines of Our Lady*. Westminster, MD: The Newmann Press, 1952.

Goyou, Georges. *Histoire Religieuse de la Nation Française*. In *The World's Great Catholic Literature*, edited by George Shuster. Garden City, NY: Halcyon House, 1942.

Graef, H.C. *The Way of the Mystics*. Cork, Ireland: The Mercier Press, Ltd., 1948.

Greenough, Patrick, OFM CONV. "The Apparitions." *Immaculata* (Jan/Feb 2002).

Gregory of Tours. *History of the Franks* in *Readings in Church History*. Edited by Coleman J. Barry, OSB. Westminster, MD: The Newman Press, 1962.

Grodecki, Louis. *Sainte-Chapelle*. Paris: Caisse Nationale Des Monuments Historiques.

Guitton, André, SSS. *Peter Julian Eymard: Apostle of the Eucharist*. Translated by Conrad Goulet. Ponteranica, Italy: Centro Eucharistico, 1996.

_____. *Peter Julian Eymard: Apostle of the Eucharist*. Paris: Mediaspaul, 1992.

Halévy, Daniel. *Péguy*. New York: Longmans, Green and Co., 1947.

Hardon, John. *Treasury of Catholic Wisdom*. San Francisco: Ignatius Press, 1987.

Holland, Robert E., sj. *Life of St. John Francis Regis*. Chicago: Loyola University Press, 1922.

Hoover, Rose F., rc, ed. *At Prayer With Saint Thérèse Couderc*. Chicago: Religious of the Cenacle, 1999.

Hilary of Poitiers. *The Trinity*. In *The Fathers of the Church*. Translated by Stephen McKenna, cssr. New York: Fathers of the Church, Inc., 1954.

The Immaculate: Special Issue on Lourdes. February 1970.

James, Bruno Scott. *St. Bernard of Clairvaux: Seen Through His Selected Letters*. Chicago: Henry Regnery Co., 1953.

Jaouen, Jean, ms. *A Grace Called La Salette*. Translated by Norman Theroux, ms. Attleboro, Mass: La Salette Publications, 1991.

Joinville, John of. *The Character of St. Louis*. Translated by René Hague. Lawrence, Kan: Coronado Press, 1968.

Julian, Philippe. *Montmartre*. Translated by Anne Carter. Oxford: Phaiden Press, 1977.

Jurgens, William A. *The Faith of the Early Fathers*, Vol. 1. Collegeville, Minn: The Liturgical Press, 1970.

John XXIII, Pope. "On The Priesthood." *Sacerdotii Nostri Primordia*. Washington, DC: National Catholic Welfare Conference, 1959.

John Paul II, Pope. "Seek the Good of the Citizens, Especially the Marginalized." *L'Osservatore Romano*. October 13, 1986.

_____. "Martyrs in the Vendée Courageously Remained Faithful to Christ's Church." *L'Osservatore Romano*. September 25, 1996.

_____. "Mary's Mediation Derives From Christ's." *L'Osservatore Romano*. October 8, 1997.

_____. "Apostolic Letter of His Holiness Pope John Paul II." *Divini Amoris Scienti*. October 19, 1997. From the website 'catolicos.org.'

_____. *France: Message of Peace, Trust, Love and Faith*. Compiled by the Daughters of St. Paul. Boston: St. Paul Editions, 1980.

Kalvelage, Bro. Francis Mary, ffi., ed. *Marian Shrines of France*. New Bedford, Mass: Franciscan Friars of the Immaculate, 1998.

Keyes, Frances Parkinson. *Bernadette of Lourdes*. Wheathampstead, England: Anthony Clarke, 1988.

Knox, Ronald. *Captive Flames*. San Francisco: Ignatius Press, 2001.

Koch, Carl. *Praying With John Baptist de la Salle*. Winona, Minn: Saint Mary's Press,

Christian Brothers Publications, 1990.

LaBarge, Margaret Wade. *Saint Louis*. Boston: Little, Brown and Company, 1968.

LaFleur, Kathryn B., SP. *St. Louise De Marillac: A Light in the Darkness*. Hyde Park, NY: New City Press, 1996.

Laurentin, René. *Bernadette Speaks*. Boston: Pauline Books & Media, 2000.

LeBrun, Charles, CJM. *The Spiritual Teaching of St. John Eudes*. Translated by Dom Basil Whelan, OSB. London, England: Sands & Co., 1934.

La Salette: The Apparition and the Message. France: The Association of Pilgrims of La Salette, 1994.

Leseur, Elisabeth. *My Spirit Rejoices*. Manchester, NH: Sophia Press, 1996.

Maguire, Mother C.E., RSCJ. *Saint Madeleine Sophie Barat*, New York: Sheed and Ward, 1960.

Manelli, Stefano M., FFI. *Jesus, Our Eucharistic Love*. New Bedford, Mass: Franciscan Friars of the Immaculate, 1996.

Maritain, Raïssa. *We Have Been Friends Together* and *Adventures in Grace*. Translated by Julie Kernan. Garden City, NY: Image Books, 1961.

McCarthy, Sr. Anna of the Sacred Heart. *St. Julie Billiart: A Saint For Our Time*. Adapted from *Rose of Picardy*. Cincinnati: Sisters of Notre Dame de Namur, 2000.

McGratty, Arthur R., SJ. *The Sacred Heart: Yesterday and Today*. New York: Benziger Brothers, Inc., 1951.

Milcent, Paul. *Jeanne Jugan: Humble, So As To Love More*. Translated by Alan Neame. London: Darton, Longman and Todd, 1981.

Miller, Malcom. *Chartres Cathedral*. United Kingdom: Pitkin Unichrome Ltd., 1996.

Montfort, Louis de. *God Alone*. Bay Shore, NY: Montfort Publications, 1999.

_____. *The Secret of the Rosary*. Translated by Mary Barbour, TOP. Bay Shore, NY: Montfort Publications, 1988.

Murphy, Francis J. *Père Jacques: Resplendent in Victory*. Washington, DC: ICS Publications, 1998.

Myers, Rawley. *The Saints Show Us Christ: Daily Readings on the Spiritual Life*. San Francisco: Ignatius Press, 1996.

'Neath St. Michael's Shield. Boston: Pauline Books & Media, 1977.

New American Bible. Saint Joseph Edition. New York: Catholic Book Publishing Co., 1992.

Northern France and the Paris Region. Clermont-Ferrand, France: Michelin, 1997.

Notre-Dame. Paris: Connaissance des Arts, 1997.

O'Brien, Bartholomew J. *The Curé of Ars: Patron Saint of Parish Priests*. Rockford, Ill: TAN Books and Publishers, Inc., 1987.

O'Connor, Patrick. *The Immaculate: Special Edition on Lourdes* (February 1970).

O'Donnell, Timothy T. *Heart of the Redeemer*. San Francisco: Ignatius Press, 1992.

O'Hanlon, M. Assumpta, OP. *St. Dominic: Servant But Friend*. St. Louis: B. Herder Book Co., 1954.

Papasogli, Benedetta. *Wisdom of the Heart: The Story of Marie Louise Trichet*. Bay Shore, NY: Montfort Publications, 1993.

Pelletier, Norman B., SSS. *Tomorrow Will Be Too Late*. Cleveland: Emmanuel Publishing, 1992.

Pernoud, Regine and Marie-Véronique Clin. *Joan of Arc: Her Story*. Translated by Jeremy duQuesnay Adams. New York: St. Martin's Press, 1999.

Pius XII, Pope. "On Devotion to the Sacred Heart." *Haurietis Aquas*. Boston: St. Paul Books & Media.

Purcell, Mary. *The World of Monsieur Vincent*. Chicago: Loyola University Press, 1989.

Ratisbonne, Theodore. *St. Bernard of Clairvaux*. Rockford, Ill: TAN Books and Publishers, Inc., 1991.

Ravier, André, SJ. *Francis de Sales: Sage and Saint*. San Francisco: Ignatius Press, 1988.

_____. *Bernadette: The Saint of Poverty and Light*. Nouvelle Librairie de France, 1974.

_____. *The Body of St. Bernadette*. Baume-les-Dames, France: Imprimé par I.M.E., 1999.

Ronan, Myles V. *S. Anne: Her Cult and Her Shrines*. London: Sands and Co., 1927.

Ruggles, Robin. *Apparition Shrines: Places of Pilgrimage and Prayer*. Boston: Pauline Books & Media, 2000.

Russell, John. *Paris*. New York: Harry N. Abrams, 1983.

Rutler, George William. *St. John Vianney: The Curé of D'Ars Today*. San Francisco: Ignatius Press, 1988.

Sacré-Coeur de Montmartre. Villeurbanne, France: Lescuyer, 1997.

St. Julie Billiart: A Saint for Our Time. Adapted from *Rose of Picardy* by Sr. Anna of the Sacred Heart McCarthy, SND de N. Cincinnati: Sisters of Notre Dame de Namur, 2000.

Saint Louis, King of France. London: Sands & Co., 1913.

Sales, Francis de. *Golden Counsels of Saint Francis de Sales*. Edited by Mary Paula McCarthy, VHM and Mary Grace McCormack, VHM. Translated by Peronne Marie Thibert, VHM. St. Louis: Monastery of the Visitation, 1994.

_____. *The Sermons of St. Francis de Sales For Advent and Christmas*. Edited by Lewis S. Fiorelli, OSFS. Translated by the Nuns of the Visitation. Rockford, Ill: TAN Books and Publishers Inc., 1987.

_____. *The Sermons of St. Francis de Sales For Lent*. Edited by Lewis S. Fiorelli, OSFS. Translated by the Nuns of the Visitation. Rockford, Ill: TAN Books and Publishers Inc., 1987.

_____. *Thy Will Be Done: Letters to Persons in the World*. Manchester, NH: Sophia Institute Press, 1995.

_____. *An Introduction to the Devout Life*. Rockford, IL: TAN Books and Publishers, 1994.

Sargent, Daniel. *Four Independents*. New York: Sheed and Ward, 1935.

Sharkey, Don. *The Woman Shall Conquer*. Libertyville, IL: Prow Books/Franciscan Marytown Press, 1976.

The Sixteen Documents of Vatican II and the Instruction on the Liturgy. Boston: St. Paul Editions.

Snyder, James. *Medieval Art*. New York, NY: Harry N. Abrams, Inc., 1989.

Soubirous, Bernadette. *Some of Bernadette's Sayings*. Nevers, France: Saint-Gildard Convent.

_____. *Personal Notes*. Baumes-les-Dames, France: Moderne l'Est, 1990.

Sylvain, Abbé Charles. *Life of Reverend Father Hermann*. Translated by Mrs. F. Raymond-Barker. New York: P.J. Kenedy & Sons, 1925.

Talbot, Francis, SJ. *Saint Among Savages: The Life of Isaac Jogues*. New York: Harper & Brothers Publishers, 1935.

Temko, Allan. *Notre-Dame of Paris*. New York: The Viking Press, 1955.

Thérèse of Lisieux. *Story of a Soul*. Translated by John Clarke, OCD. Washington, DC: ICS Publications, 1976.

_____. *The Prayers of Saint Thérèse of Lisieux*. Translated by Aletheia Kane, OCD. Washington: ICS Publications, 1997.

The Trial of St. Joan of Arc. The verbatim report of the proceedings from the Orleans Manuscript. Translated by W.S. Scott. London: The Folio Society, 1968.

Trochu, Francis. *Curé D'Ars: A Biography of St. Jean-Marie Vianney*. Translated by Ronald Matthews. Manila, Philippines: Sinag Tala Publishers, Inc., 1998.

Van Dam, Raymond. *Saints and Their Miracles in Antique Gaul*. Princeton: Princeton University Press, 1993.

Van Thuan, Francis Xavier Nguyen. *Testimony of Hope*. Boston: Pauline Books & Media, 2000.

Veras, Richard. "To Quell the Terror." *Magnificat* (July 2002).

Watkin, E.I. *Neglected Saints*. San Francisco: Ignatius Press. Originally Published in 1955.

Yeo, Margaret. *These Three Hearts*. Milwaukee: The Bruce Publishing Co., 1940.